Creating a
Learning Environment

An Educational Leader's Guide to
Managing School Culture

John M. Brucato

ScarecrowEducation
Lanham, Maryland • Toronto • Oxford
2005

Published in the United States of America
by ScarecrowEducation
An imprint of The Rowman & Littlefield Publishing Group, Inc.
4501 Forbes Boulevard, Suite 200, Lanham, Maryland 20706
www.scarecroweducation.com

PO Box 317
Oxford
OX2 9RU, UK

British Library Cataloguing in Publication Information Available

Library of Congress Cataloging-in-Publication Data

Brucato, John M., 1955–
   Creating a learning environment : an educational leader's guide to
managing school culture / John M. Brucato.
     p. cm.
   ISBN 1-57886-190-X (pbk. : alk. paper)
   1. School management and organization—United States. 2. School
environment—United States. 3. Educational leadership—United States.
I. Title.

LB2805.B825 2005
371.2—dc22

                                                          2004014854

♾™ The paper used in this publication meets the minimum requirements of
American National Standard for Information Sciences—Permanence of
Paper for Printed Library Materials, ANSI/NISO Z39.48-1992.
Manufactured in the United States of America.

To my colleagues who have chosen a career in educational leadership; the warriors, martyrs, and idealists who manage to hold the line while having minimal resources with which to fend off relentless attacks from multiple fronts.

For my wife, Linda, a cancer survivor, who has taught me strength and how to live in the now. To my children, Jonathan, Jake, and Gianna and the terriers Hope and Gus, who remind me that play is as important as work. To my parents, Connie and Charlie, who taught me the value of an education, hard work, and respect.

To my office manager, Dee, and my mentors, Bronkie, Bardol, Marilyn, Don, Tom, Ralph, Dennis, and the Duke.

Contents

Foreword

This book is not, in any sense of the word, the product of formal educational research. It is, rather, the expression of a belief developed during a long career in the field of public education. This belief is centered upon the schoolhouse and its role in determining the end result of the process that is carried on within its walls and in its ancillary functions.

Human beings are affected by their heredity and their environment. The former is beyond the scope of even the most determined theorist. It is, therefore, in the latter area that educators can do the most to provide the best possible start in life to those entrusted to them. It is my firm belief, as it is Mr. Brucato's, that the climate of the schoolhouse, in its physical presence, the level and nature of its expectations, and the comfort of its students is the prime factor in meeting this challenge.

John Brucato discusses the nature of an optimum school climate, the obstacles that can operate to hinder its achievement, and the steps that can be taken by an administrator and a staff in making it happen.

There is much here of value.

Phillip F. Flaherty

Preface: A New Century for The American Schoolhouse!

A national, longitudinal study of 72,000 teen-aged students, who were followed from grade seven to grade twelve, was released in April 2002. The report of this study makes very compelling reading for all American educators.

These researchers found that a good classroom, managed by caring adults, is "the single most important" factor affecting students' sense of well being. Such a classroom thus had a major effect upon the likelihood of their engaging in any behaviors that put their health at risk.

"School environment has a much bigger impact on what happens to kids than what is taught in the school," concluded Robert Blum in a University of Minnesota study released in 2001.

Isn't it time that we started paying closer attention to School Culture?

Acknowledgments

First, I thank Mr. Phil Flaherty, assistant director of the Massachusetts Secondary School Administrators Association and editor of *The Leader,* the journal of Massachusetts middle and high school administration. Without Phil's encouragement and willingness to revise and edit my manuscript, this book would never have been completed.

I would also like to thank Mr. Jose Pinto for his technological genius in getting the book ready for print.

In addition, I wish to thank my assistants, Rick Porter and Nancy Angelini, for their dedication, loyalty, and commitment in driving the numerous school culture reform initiatives we have introduced at Milford High School.

Introduction

When "Breaking Ranks: Changing an American Institution," a comprehensive report including six main themes and eighty-one specific recommendations, was released in 1986, radical educational reform initiatives would follow. Although the report was focused exclusively on reshaping the American high school for the purpose of bringing about high achievement for all, students, teachers, and educators at every level would feel the impact.

As the industrialized model of schooling, which has remained in place for over a century, was replaced by a model more suitable for the information age, it became essential for "old dogs" to learn "new tricks." While teachers would be forced to reckon with unfamiliar teaching methodologies, assessment practices, and curricula framed around new standards and learning strands, school leaders would be left with the difficult task of supervising the process.

In theory, school administrators would be given more authority to run their schools while overseeing the professional growth of their instructors. In practice, however, school leaders were given more responsibilities without the needed resources and autonomy to meet the expectations of educational reform. More importantly, school leaders would be forced into roles, which would diminish their ability to "manage the schoolhouse." For the past two plus decades, embattled school leaders have worked harder for less, while left alone and responsible for a new breed of oppositional students, entitled parents, and disgruntled teachers, micromanaging school boards, dictatorial superintendents, dysfunctional boards of education, and business leaders who think public schools can be run like the private workplace.

The cries of school leaders nationally simply have not been heard. While most anyone asked would agree that the job of an American public school administrator is dangerously stressful and thankless, there have been few who have come forward to champion the cause of this dying breed of educators.

To complicate matters further, many educational leadership programs sponsored by colleges and universities to properly prepare and certify aspiring administrators have failed miserably. This is understandable given the fact that these programs are heavily laden with course work grounded to educational philosophy, research, and pedagogy. Useful and practical courses designed to help aspiring administrators survive the job by addressing the countless issues related to school culture are few and far between.

The vast majority of school leaders who are now counting their days to retirement are former teachers, coaches, activity advisors, and athletic directors who had the opportunity to transition into administrative roles within the same environment that reared them. As the role of a school leader became less appealing and more difficult, fewer educators suitable for these roles have been willing to step into the fire. This being the case, the already-shallow pool of both qualified and aspiring school leaders continues to shrink.

More significantly, those who remain in the pool are looking at short-lived careers for those reasons already established and one more reason with which we should be most concerned. School leaders are now moving from one school district to another at an alarming rate. In doing so, many are doomed to fail as they arrive in school districts with unfamiliar cultures requiring the kind of nurturing that may very well be elusive to them. The few remaining administrators who have moved up through the ranks in their existing school district are often left as scapegoats while their predecessors either leave under fire or retire before they have had an opportunity to properly mentor their successor into the role.

Examining the results of educational reform since "Breaking Ranks," there is good news and bad. The good news is that educators nationally are more accountable for student learning and our young people are better prepared. Curricula are developed with specific standards in mind, and the high-stakes testing that follows the rigorous standards-based instruction confirms our growth through the achievement of our students. Reform initiatives have sent our teachers back to school while demanding more of those aspiring to become teachers before they are awarded a license to teach.

The bad news, however, is that in meeting these ends, school leaders, who have shouldered the burden of responsibility for ensuring that the job gets done, have paid the price.

My motivation for writing this book derives from the choices I have made and the revelations I have experienced as a modern-day school administrator who believes that there is, in fact, a pathway to survival, success, and enjoyment in the role of a school leader. The pathway to which I refer is one that will forever keep you focused on meeting the needs of young people, while nurturing relationships with all of the stakeholders responsible for bringing this to fruition. It is a pathway with several steps:

- To successfully manage a schoolhouse, a leader must define his or her purpose as it relates to the culture of that schoolhouse.
- Second, the leader must determine if he or she is a good match for the chosen institution. This can only be accomplished through a thorough, intensive self-examination.
- Finally, the leader must be committed to collaborating with fellow school leaders who have roots in similar cultures so as to make informed decisions on cultural reform initiatives.

The material I have compiled in this manuscript is representative of what I have learned from successful educational leaders and significant others who place people first and the three P's (policies, programs, politics) second. It is my hope that the sharing of my experiences will inspire you to do the same with your colleagues and significant others. To become an effective autonomous school leader, one must learn from those educational leaders who have become successful through their ability to both manage people and school culture.

Therefore, this book, which is anecdotal in nature, is designed to inspire educational leaders, and for that matter, anyone who believes that managing the culture of our schools should become the driving force behind future educational reform initiatives.

There are no "how-to" guides or recipes for success that will help you become a school leader capable of better posturing young people for success. Your ability to make a difference lies in your resolve to be true to yourself while following the lead of those colleagues who can show you the way through their experience, courage, and conviction.

Part I

THE PROBLEM

In public education today, we would be hard pressed to identify a single school district that hasn't changed gears to meet the demands of a reform movement insisting that we change the way we think about education. Changes in philosophy and pedagogy coupled with curriculum revision and new instructional methodology have school administrators reeling. Many have opted for early retirement, while those left behind try to play "Beat the Clock!" For those few educational leaders left in a shallow pool that's rapidly drying up, taking on the responsibility of running a new school or district often becomes a game of "Survivor." There is, however, no million-dollar prize for keeping your job after the token three-year Cinderella period is over.

"Where do I begin?" asks the Messiah who wins the job by convincing the selection committee that he is, in fact, the chosen one. Of course, he asks this question of himself while looking at stacks of books, manuals, files, proposals, budget ledgers, and spreadsheets piled high on the desk of his not-so-pristine new office, a place that will soon be called home.

A complete analysis of test results might be a good place to start, but then again, a wise man would learn as much about the budget first to determine if dollars have, in fact, been spent and accounted for properly. This, however, would prove foolhardy until all policy manuals were read and understood. The mission statement and how it relates to learning outcomes is a logical starting point, but that automatically raises the question of what is being done in the area of assessment. Assessment must be directly linked to learning standards addressed in coherently written curriculums, which are properly scoped and sequenced. Any decent school administrator knows that it's diverse programming, not curriculum, that promulgates educational opportunities for all students, so this is clearly where one begins.

With the preliminary game plan ready to be set in motion, this administrator has his "revelation." He remembers everything he learned as a teacher, coach, mentor, and someone fortunate enough to play on a team or two while growing up. It's not programs but people who create and sustain learning opportunities for others. By investing in a complete understanding of the culture of the district and determining what is productive or unproductive about it, the educational leader knows that in order to get anything done, he needs to know everything he can about the strengths and weaknesses of the players.

The climate in each and every school building is determined by the culture, which becomes clearly identified through its leadership. Is the chain of command understood and followed by teachers and staff? Is each and every working member of the school accountable for performing their job with excellence? Do teachers maintain lofty but reasonable standards and model the very behaviors they require of their students, or is there a double standard? Are administrators clear in their expectations of teachers and staff? Are they good role models who gain the trust of all members of the school community through their consistency in dealing with issues? Do students, faculty, and staff feel safe in their building? Do teachers serve the needs of all students or only those who are not skill deficient or emotionally needy? Is the mission of the school clearly articulated in all curricular areas and cocurricular programs? Is mutual respect and respect for diversity demanded of all with no exceptions, or does it matter who you are? Most importantly, do teachers and staff members like coming to work each day? Do they enjoy their relationships with colleagues and students or are they chronic in their complaints and criticisms?

When climate is synchronized with culture there are countless hours saved on the planning and implementation of programs and initiatives that require invested individuals to ensure their success. When the climate is right, administrators make progress with deficient instructors who clearly understand the consequences of their reluctance to improve. Constructive criticism becomes a useful intervention where those in need accept it without resentment or becoming emotionally un-done. When climate becomes a focal point for administrators, mean-spirited behavior on the part of teachers is not accepted and is dealt with accordingly.

When dealing with discipline problems, teachers must understand that they will be part of the solution and that it's not the job of the administrator to give them their "pound of flesh." Climate-focused schools buy into reform as it meets the needs of the school community and not because it's trendy or "the thing to do." These institutions are orderly and well organized and their leaders insistent that all constituents understand process, procedures, and protocol while properly communicating their needs, concerns, and frustrations. Ill feelings among faculty, students, and staff are not allowed to fester while conflicts are regularly mediated in a timely manner. The students in these schools are invested because they have a voice, are treated consistently, and are clear in what is expected of them.

If it's starting to sound like a utopia, consider what needs to happen in order to get there. To begin with, changing the culture of a school or school district is far more difficult than putting together programs and developing policies. It's a difficult job where the leader or CEO must have a clear vision, uncompromising conviction and ice in his veins, while accepting the reality that in order to change things, he will forever be mired in controversy. Unlike the leaders that John W. Gardner described a decade ago, this is an altogether different individual with a style all his own. After all, it's not as if he got to pick his own team. This is where education differs from other organizations, and why Total Quality Management (TQM) is a useful tool in the business world, but often a waste of time for school leaders. What do you do with incompetent, lazy, sarcastic teachers that you didn't hire and have glowing evaluations from past administrators? How about team leaders and department heads who don't have the stomach for dealing with colleagues who need a wake-up call? These are just a couple of inherent handicaps a school leader faces when devising a plan of attack to dismantle the old culture while developing a new one at the same time.

The game plan is ambitious, requiring an individual with many of the often overlooked personal qualities and talents that result in a school system choosing the wrong leader. The scenario is common, as the few principals and superintendents left in the shallow pool of administrators for hire, have most often been somewhere else.

For this "dead pool" you can blame the unreasonable demands of the education reform movement, fueled by "A Nation at Risk," a 1983 report that exposed public education for failing to meet the needs of American children living in a different world. Or you can rationalize that many years of a strong economy have caused talented educators to both leave the field and forget about the pursuit of thankless administrative jobs that offer few benefits and no security. For whatever reason, school districts looking for viable principals and superintendents need to think long and hard about who they are looking for, but only after determining what they are looking for.

If you want mediocrity, there are plenty of "machine-like" administrators still available who can recite passages from curriculum frameworks, push papers, and skew data. Those who can be easily persuaded into making the popular decision, are eager to please everybody, and have impressive credentials can also be located. These are not, however, educational leaders. Educational leaders are climate focused and intuitive about people; they are proven team builders.

This book is not a research document but a point of view based on my experience as an educator and the methodology I have employed as an administrator. It describes the characteristics of a climate-focused educational leader and the guiding principles that can bring about school improvement through changing school culture.

CHAPTER 1

Assessing School Culture:
Putting the Horse before the Cart

School culture reform initiatives evolve out of understandings of the culture that must be thoroughly and objectively assessed. To make an objective assessment, all members of the school community must be considered as well as any other agents affiliated with the school and school district.

When new leaders take over the responsibilities of a school or district, they are, in the majority of cases, inheriting a host of individuals who will determine whether or not they are successful in their administration. They may have something to say about the demographics of their leadership team, but the teachers, staff, students, parents, and school board are a given factor. More importantly, each of these groups has key players who can be identified as such by their ability to influence both the opinion and behavior of others.

Both the homegrown leader and the leader unfamiliar with his players have equally difficult tasks. The homegrown leader knows the players, having established a history with them already. There will be those individuals unwilling to accept that their personal and professional relationship with a former coworker has to change. With many of these people the leader will be forced to take action to demonstrate the strength of his convictions. This often results in "bad blood" which can quickly infect the faculty and staff. If left unchecked, the homegrown leader's authority will be questioned and challenged from day one. The only way these negative situations can be avoided is for the leader to take the time to deal with each and every individual privately and separately. Confidentiality in these matters is critical, for newly gained trust can be destroyed with even the smallest leak of information.

The homegrown leader must also prove to his known adversaries that he is not vindictive or irreversibly ill-disposed toward them because of past differences of opinion. The most important thing, however, that this administrator will do is to prove himself to be an educational leader who can hold his own in the political arena. Politics, like it or not, has everything to do with this leader's rise to power. His political savvy will determine early on if he has the mettle to hold true to his convictions and the ability to stand firm on his platform. Resisting political pressure will become the "acid test" that will determine whether or not he is successful in changing the school culture. These tests will come early and often, leaving no room for error or misjudgment. In knowing the players, this leader resolves that each and every decision he makes will be unpopular for some. For those in opposition to his dispositions, the administrator will demand only two things: consistency and rationale. The first time he succumbs to political pressure and contradicts himself, he loses credibility. Without credibility, he may survive his administration, but he will not change the culture.

I am a homegrown principal, having taught fifteen years at my school and served another five as assistant principal before taking the helm four years ago. I knew what I was getting myself into, and had a clear understanding about what I wanted to accomplish and what had to be done in order for me to move our school forward. As a former teacher, coach, and student leadership advisor, I had the good fortune of developing meaningful relationships with my students, while contributing to all aspects of their educational development. As an assistant principal, I built up my reputation as an administrator by becoming a strong disciplinarian in a school, in which, at that time, the "inmates were running the asylum." Like most of my colleagues, in my many years in the classroom I was disgruntled about administrative inconsistencies and resentful of the fact that I had little input in the educational reform process of our school.

We were typical of any large, suburban high school where it was business as usual. Our large physical plant made it convenient for teachers to remain isolated from one another, while remaining closely affiliated only with the members of their department. Conflicts and in-fighting between the departments was commonplace, and our two-house system often pitted one assistant principal against the other.

Bimonthly faculty meetings were a circus. These regularly scheduled "gripe sessions" were as entertaining as they were perverse. Needless to say, little was accomplished in terms of making us more efficient at doing our jobs. Our culture was clearly defined through the climate of these meetings, which was often hostile and indicative of poor morale among the faculty. Support staff was never included in our meetings, as those staff members were treated as second-class citizens in our school. Differences of opinion between administrators served to further fragment the faculty, as different teachers would support the efforts of certain administrators for both personal gain and protective insulation.

Student discipline was administered inconsistently within the houses, causing a poor climate throughout the student body. Oppositional students took advantage of the rifts in administration and seized every opportunity to wreak havoc on the school and on specific teachers, who rarely were given the needed support. Vandalism in the school was commonplace, as was smoking in the lavatories and stairwells. Drug use was rarely addressed and bullying and harassment within the student population was yet another negative defining characteristic of our school culture. Teacher's union grievances were common and faculty absenteeism chronic.

What I found especially discouraging and unproductive during these times was the observation/evaluation process to which teachers were subjected. I don't remember ever becoming more reflective about my teaching or improving my methods as a result of administrative observations, but it was certainly a good opportunity to improve on my acting skills. I can remember the entire process hitting rock bottom when one of our former superintendents decided to introduce the "Madeline Hunter Model." What a paradox! There we were, in the lowest depths of school climate, and now we were being evaluated on "feeling tone" in our classrooms!

In spite of our culture, there was good teaching going on by those instructors who enjoyed teaching and working with young adults. I'm sure I did my part to contribute to our undesirable climate, but I am proud to say that I never cheated my students out of one day of education, and I rarely took a day off. Fortunately for me, discipline problems were few and far between. To turn any of my problems over to the administration, I viewed as a failure on my part.

When I became an assistant principal, I was determined to win the support of my colleagues by proving myself as a strong disciplinarian and teacher-friendly administrator. I was also on a planned mission to change the way students were behaving in the school. There were a number of defining moments for me while in this role and many days were very lonely. I did, however, gain invaluable administrative experience, as a new principal arrived in time to begin moving us in a new direction. Don was a jovial, visible principal who spent little time in the office and gave me the autonomy I required to run my house the way I wanted. He taught me that discipline gets old very quickly, and that aspiring administrators must be well-read educators and risk takers. He schooled me in every aspect of the principalship while challenging me to develop myself as an educational leader. From this man, I learned the intricacies of school scheduling. When we launched our campaign to bring semester block scheduling to Milford High School, we fought the battle together and made it a reality. He gave me the professional development responsibility, so it was my job to ensure that our teachers were ready to make the transition to extended learning time classes. My research and the pursuit of quality programs for our teachers resulted in my coaxing the principal, who had authored a number of education journal articles, to coauthor "Questions and Answers about Block Scheduling" (*Eye on Education*, 1999) with me. This was a significant undertaking that became a reality mostly because of his experience and expertise, and my enthusiasm.

Don and I had our differences in philosophy, especially where student discipline was concerned, but he was an excellent mentor who helped me to define myself as an administrator, while learning hands-on about all aspects of the principalship. In return, I gave him my unwavering loyalty and support.

When he decided to move on, he had succeeded in leaving his mark on the school, while setting the table for me. His promise to me from the start, to make me capable of running the school in his absence by giving me the opportunity to learn, grow, and develop, would, in turn, be my promise to all of my future assistants.

Part II

BEGINNINGS

The newcomer administrator, coming to a well-established school like ours, faces an entirely different set of challenges in moving a school forward.

First and foremost, he must gain the answers to all of the key questions before deciding if, in fact, he wants to subject himself to such an ambitious undertaking. Educational leaders looking to make monumental changes in an organization are success-driven, autonomous, self-guided individuals who believe they can outwork anyone in the business. They must first, however, carefully assess the culture and the history that defines it.

CHAPTER 2

The Six Key Questions to Assessing School Culture

QUESTION 1: DID SOMEONE FROM WITHIN THE SYSTEM APPLY FOR THIS JOB?

For the climate-focused leader, the answer to this question could determine whether or not he takes the job. Internal candidates who have been passed over can be very dangerous individuals indeed. What measures they will take to make the life of the new administrator difficult will depend upon how bitter they are. Who is the internal candidate aligned with? Who are his friends in the community? Why was he passed over? How do key people in the school community view him or her? Without the answers to these questions, the incoming leader leaves himself vulnerable to a host of problems that can surface at critical times in his administration. By dealing with this issue up front, the incoming leader will not need to be concerned with looking over his shoulder. A more significant intervention, however, involves acknowledging the feelings of the unhappy runner-up while at the same time seizing the opportunity to make clear your expectations for him. This is an important but often-avoided confrontation that can result in the undermining of a good leader. Making a friend out of a potential adversary right from the start, or at least making a bona fide attempt to do so, can be a small success that can make possible many more critical future victories.

QUESTION 2: IS THE CHAIN OF COMMAND WELL DEFINED AND FOLLOWED BY ALL STAFF MEMBERS OF THE SCHOOL OR DISTRICT?

Every organization has procedural manuals and protocol to follow, but before investing the time in learning these "ropes," it is wise for one to first determine if what is written, is in fact gospel. Ask first if protocol is respected and understood before going to the books. It's a well-known fact that in the business of education we have a policy for just about everything. Each time we encounter a new situation not covered by existing policy, we create a new one. In addition, we are forever amending and revising existing policies in attempts to increase our efficiency. Knowledge of the realities of the chain of command gives us critical knowledge of the culture with which we are dealing, and can easily be considered our most useful cultural assessment tool (see figure 2.1). Take for example, the system in which certain individuals are allowed to circumvent the chain of command to get what they want or need, such as an influential parent talking to the superintendent about his child's problem with a teacher without first speaking with the teacher or a school administrator. Better still, consider the teacher who has an audience with school board members to protest his or her teaching assignment prior to discussing it with the principal or superintendent. Finally, there is the all-too-common scenario of a faction of teachers who are negligent in enforcing school policies, making it difficult for both students and their more diligent colleagues who "toe the mark" to perform to the best of their ability. These are just a few of the hundreds of problems with which administrators spend countless hours dealing, concerning situations in which there are different expectations for different individuals. It will be no easy task in changing this aspect of school culture, but you can rest assure that as long as it is allowed to continue, the climate will not change. In choosing ones battles, this is one that must be fought, as a loss here will make all future endeavors futile.

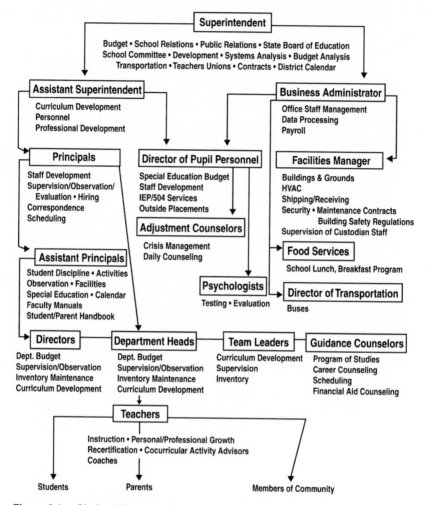

Figure 2.1.   Chain of Command

QUESTION 3: HOW ARE TEACHERS, ADMINISTRATORS, AND SUPPORT STAFF HIRED?

With many (*all* in my home state of Massachusetts) school boards to-day limited in their authority to do anything other than hire superin-tendents, oversee budget, and see that policies are adopted, revised, and enforced, there should be little or no intervention where the hiring of school personnel is concerned. Similarly, the superintendent who hires

principals should be giving them the autonomy in staffing their buildings, while at the same time supporting the initiatives of principals to
dismiss negligent and underperforming employees. School law today,
as it relates to the hiring and dismissal of school personnel, is in most
cases, better defined than it was in the past and one need only look to
statutes published by each of our individual states to confirm this fact.
Many school systems, however, continue to follow traditional employment methods that may in fact be contradictory to the law. Therefore,
it is critical to know what the proper procedures are and if they are in
fact being followed by the school district.

The prospective administrator should also know in advance if it is
expected by the school board and superintendent that their requests to
hire certain individuals for certain positions will in fact be honored.
School leaders who succumb to pressure to make political appoint-
ments can never assert themselves as autonomous administrators. Instead, they further perpetuate a tradition that reinforces the compla-
cency in a culture ruled by the "It's not what you know, but who you
know" doctrine. It's difficult enough having to accept an existing personnel roster you had nothing to do with, but having to add additional
individuals to the mix who are not of your choosing makes it unlikely
that the culture will ever change. When school personnel know that the
mission of their superior is to hire the most qualified individual for
each and every position, their behavior changes almost immediately.
Moving a veteran staff in a different direction is especially difficult, as
habits and attitudes have been cemented over time. By proving from
the outset that he will pick his own players and deploy them accordingly, the school leader removes the very insulation that has resulted in
mediocrity and resistance among faculty and staff members who believe that they are untouchable.

QUESTION 4: WHAT DOES THE PHYSICAL PLANT LOOK LIKE?

Clean buildings that are well maintained and kept up to date have
everything to do with teaching and learning. Show me a run-down
building that is dirty and not properly furnished or equipped and I will
usually be able to show you an underperforming school.

If lavatories and classrooms aren't kept clean and sanitary or graffiti is left to deface corridor walls, one can draw a number of accurate conclusions about the culture of the school and district. To begin with, students who take pride in their building exert an enormous amount of pressure on the undesirable minority looking for opportunities to perform this type of defacement of school property.

Teachers whose individual classrooms are kept neat, well organized, and free of clutter are likely to be well prepared and more than likely will prove to be effective educators. One look at a teacher's desk will tell you something about his work ethic. Stacks of paper, books, and other clutter covered in a blanket of dust reveal the work ethic and consequent reputation of that teacher prior to any introductions.

To determine if the maintenance staff has a "sweetheart" deal, simply look in corners, under, above, and on top of furnishings, in storage closets, lavatories, and especially, assess the condition of the window glass. If dust, dirt, cobwebs, smudges, smears, and week-old dried-up beverage stains are commonplace, you are looking at the work of a custodial staff used to doing the bare minimum. Building aesthetics is one of the most often overlooked variables in school climate while telling an important story about the commitment of the district to create the best learning environment possible. The condition of the building will also have a significant impact on attracting the best new teachers available, who will continue to have multiple employment opportunities as the national teacher shortage escalates.

The argument that budget constraints are to blame for run-down facilities does not hold water. Keeping a building clean and well maintained on a regular basis does not usually cost extra money. It *does* take planning, a conscience, and a clear understanding that everyone on board will perform their duties according to specifications. Therefore, building maintenance issues are the responsibility of the building leadership. Climate-/culture-directed leaders always make building aesthetics a priority. Not only are their buildings well maintained, but they showcase many visible symbols and indicators of student accomplishments and progress. Bulletin boards are covered and maintained, while students' work is displayed regularly, along with the usual championship banners and trophies. The mission statement is visible to all, and yes, there's an American flag in every classroom. The Milford High School Mission Statement, for example, is as follows:

> The mission of Milford High School is to provide an educational process in a safe environment that will foster critical thinking and the acquisition of knowledge and skills: a self-discipline that will encourage academic excellence, self-sufficiency and personal responsibility; and a respect for diversity, all of which will prepare students for lifelong learning as well as establish a high standard of ethics and a willingness to make a positive contribution to society.

QUESTION 5: HOW DO STUDENTS, FACULTY, AND STAFF INTERACT IN THE SCHOOL COMMUNITY?

Students are painfully honest about their teachers and school and far too often they are not given the time or opportunity to evaluate their teachers. Speaking with a healthy cross section of students from different grade levels, academic and cocurricular interests, and leadership roles in the school will give an educational leader a wealth of information. Students will tell you emphatically whether or not the faculty as a whole treats them fairly and consistently. Additionally, they will reveal the identities of those individual instructors whom they feel are closed-minded, ill prepared, mean-spirited, and inconsistent. While it's true that different students respond differently to different methods, it is easy to determine whom they respect. A stern, business-like instructor who teaches with a fire and passion for the subject almost invariably earns the respect of the students in the same way the more flamboyant stage performer does, by modeling commitment and responsibility for them. If the "Do as I say, not as I do" philosophy is the prevailing ethos of the faculty, the students will quickly alert you to this cultural reality.

The faculty can be just as revealing in their analysis of both their students and colleagues. The ones who have the least to say are usually the best sources of information. Those who see nothing but good, lack a firm grip on reality, while the remaining prophets of doom reveal themselves as the most dangerous teachers in the school. Simple mathematics can be employed to draw an important conclusion about faculty morale. If the number of apparent malcontents on the faculty is equal to or greater than those who are seem content and secure in their role, you have a ton of work to do in shifting the balance the other way. The first step in the process will be to root out the most venomous of the malcontents and formulate a plan that will prevent them from crippling and infecting others.

The support staff, especially office managers and technical assistants, is another overlooked source of information and, in my opinion, one of the most important driving forces of a healthy school culture. These individuals are the lifeblood of the school as they deal with everyone from belligerent students to rude parents to uncooperative teachers. I prefer to use the title "office manager" instead of secretary, because the job has become just as difficult and involved as that of the school administrators. If these people aren't treated like the valuable staff members they are, their performance will be subpar and school administrators will pay the price. Interviews with support staff members will reveal how well their responsibilities are defined and how they view themselves in the school community. If office staff feel like subordinates, are given no opportunity to be innovative with office management practices, and are not appreciated for their efforts, school leaders will be doing much more work than they have to. More importantly, if the leadership allows faculty, students, and parents to take advantage of and abuse staff members, then the ability of the support staff to make a significant impact on improved building climate is further diminished.

The following chapters on students, teachers, and staff offer a number of suggestions for giving these various members of the school community opportunities to become more invested in the school while feeling better about themselves and their contemporaries.

QUESTION 6: HOW DO PARENTS AND OTHER MEMBERS OF THE COMMUNITY VIEW THEIR SCHOOL?

The school leader needs to pay an equal amount of attention to how the school is perceived as he does with the reality of how it is run. Students, we know, tell tales out of school. Much of what is heard in the home and around the community is taken as gospel. If the school or district is viewed as a closed shop where parents are "locked out" and kept in the dark on reform initiatives, then, more than likely, school leaders are spending a lot of time doing battle with parents. Poor lines of communication can easily be identified as the culprit, but before any attempts can be made to repair the damage, one must first determine how and when communication broke down.

One possible general answer can be applied to many American public schools that have experienced rapid turnover of school leaders. When the national education reform movement surfaced some fifteen years ago, school districts everywhere were forced to make significant changes in a business that had been doing things differently, and sometimes obscurely, for the prior ninety years. Administrators incapable of enduring the shock wave were either forced into early retirement or dismissed. Replacement administrators have, in many cases, survived only short tenures, as impatient districts have offered little security in one, two, and three year contracts.

The more often administrations turn over, the less likely school leaders are to gain any footing in the community. With parents, especially, left out of the loop, lines of communication are severed. With poor communication, rumors run rampant and school leaders fight an uphill battle in making improvements—that is, if they can stay around long enough to attempt to do so.

Parental and community support, if not sought and achieved from the outset, will never develop, and this diminishes any hope of the school leader's ability to change the culture and move the school forward. If, in fact, it is determined that parents view the school negatively, the school leader must be prepared to spend a lot of time with parents to determine what the concerns are and how they will be addressed. Visibility in the community will be critical as will be making and keeping public speaking engagements. Keeping in mind that parents and community members elect school committees, the possibilities for school reform and especially cultural reform are endless without the support of key parents and community leaders. Charting out the significant agencies in the community can be helpful in ensuring that all members of the community are considered and included. (See figure 2.2.)

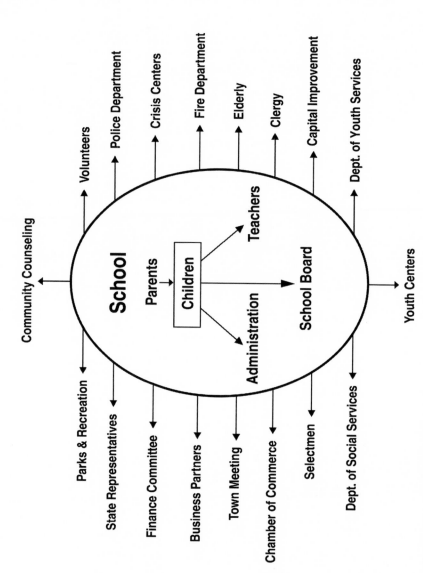

Figure 2.2.   Charting the Community

CHAPTER 3

Why We Need to Read, Write, and Reflect: The Journal

All effective educational leaders are well versed in the art of psychotherapy. What we all learned in Psychology I is that in order to help others with their resolve, we must first understand ourselves.

In the business of educational administration today, performing our daily assortment of responsibilities leaves us little time to read about the very issues with which we spend countless hours dealing. If we don't remain well informed, we run the risk of misrepresenting ourselves and losing credibility as professionals. Writing about what we do gives us the opportunity to reflect and learn from our practices. By being reflective we minimize our tendency to be reactive. When embroiled in a high-level, emotionally charged, controversial issue, a step back and good hard look within can make the difference between a successful resolution or a bad decision that can diminish or cripple your administration.

During the 2000–2001 school year I had the good fortune of joining fellow principals within our district in a collaborative leadership course that we designed. This is where I met Dr. Ralph Edwards, the Harvard University professor assigned to teach our course. Ralph is a highly respected, renowned educator who has done it all, from teaching in the New York City schools to serving as a principal in Harlem, during the most difficult years of urban public education.

If you met Ralph, you couldn't help but be inspired, as he talks about education in a way that every "trench warrior" can understand and appreciate it. While understanding the importance for us to vent on those issues we found frustrating, he managed to convince us that we must stay poised and focused on moving our schools forward by investing our energies and talents on those things we can directly control, independent of the district. Under Dr. Edward's guidance, we spent time visiting one another's schools and then talking about the education we witnessed. It also gave us an opportunity to share observations, an opportunity, which we seldom, if ever, are afforded.

Ralph discussed the importance of journal writing and critical assessment of selected educational journal articles. Understanding that we had little time to read and process major works, Ralph selected some short but important readings for us.

The best part of our experience, however, evolved from having the opportunity to bond as colleagues and share expertise and experiences with one another. This, I believe, is how we grow professionally as educators. The scheduled demands of each and every day keep us in isolation from one another. Surely, we may attend conferences or seminars to listen to "dog and pony" shows offered up by well-paid consultants, some of whom never taught a day in the classroom or ran a school. But these events will serve only to fuel our resentment.

Our opportunities to spend time with fellow school leaders where our experiences drive the agenda are limited, as is the case with some of our teachers who have never seen the inside of another classroom while a lesson is in progress. If we don't collaborate with our colleagues or see what's going on in other school buildings, then how can we assess our own progress? If we make high-stakes testing the means to every end, then we again become the victims of our own actions, don't we? If we demand that our teachers engage in professional growth activities, we must do the same. By demonstrating for them, through our own experiences, the importance of becoming reflective as well as collegial we are increasing the probability of their becoming better educators.

I do not like educational jargon, pedagogy, philosophy, or politics. Like many of you, I am insulted by the educational consultants who have never taught but pontificate on various points of view. I'm not impressed with research or data on some trumpeted educational methods that may have reformed some rural high school in the Midwest. I am not a conformist and radical only in my points of view that relate to helping the students of my school become more successful. I am certainly not a prophet and my school has no fewer problems than yours, I'm sure. We have all been exposed to the same movements and we've been told to pick our battles where the national education reform movement is concerned. We've been told regularly to forget about this or that because we just won't win. (Come now, the New England Patriots defeated the St. Louis Rams in a game they couldn't win.)

Each of our school communities is different. The needs of our students cannot be generalized. What works in one place may be an abject failure in another. What we have in common, however, is our human nature, courage, vulnerability, instability, conviction, compassion, passion, and determination. We need one another for confirmation of what we do and can never allow ourselves to lose track of why we do it. We work in one of the most difficult professions our nation offers.

We have to deal with adults, young adults, children, and teachers who at any given time can be any of the three. If we don't know what motivates them, then we can't inspire them. If we can't inspire them, chances are we can't change their behavior. This business is about people, their hearts and souls.

If we don't talk about people and dynamics, idiosyncrasies, persuasions, preoccupations, and personalities and how they interact in our school communities, then we can't influence people to bring about needed change. A good educator turning incompetent happens for a reason. Somewhere along the way he loses his soul, no longer appreciating the intrinsic rewards that once sustained him. When an educator loses his soul, loss of personal pride and self-respect are soon to follow. This is not "teacher burnout," as much as it is a debilitating and insidious disease that infiltrates all public school systems, finds its victims, and slowly works to drain that person of the pleasure and satisfaction once felt from teaching and caring for young people.

This is why I write and how this book became a reality. In sharing with you my experiences, I am reflecting on my practices and staying focused on what I need to do with people, not paper, in order to make a difference in the education of our young people. It is only through self-assessment that we can learn the truth.

"CONFESSIONS OF A SECONDARY SCHOOL PRINCIPAL": OR, ONE SIZE FITS ALL

Journal writing, you know, is spontaneous, reflective, honest, heartfelt, and at times therapeutic. In writing my last entry, I had a notion or maybe it was just a daydream. We principals are prone to those impromptu lapses of consciousness that are welcomed distractions to the day.

What if the high school principals across the nation all made journal entries online at the same time on a dozen or so days throughout the school year and some computer wizard took all the entries and found the common themes, likes, dislikes, hostilities, frustrations, etc.? Would we in fact learn anything that we didn't already know? Would we be enlightened, motivated, stimulated, or even curious? Would we feel better about the job because we discovered a new-found bond with colleagues everywhere? Perhaps we could learn a coping strategy not yet discovered—but it's not very likely.

We are the martyrs (champions), my friends, and we'll keep on fighting to the end! Fighting for what becomes the question, Is it perspective that we seek, or the constant need for new and impossible challenges? Foolish pride and principals go together, so perhaps this can be the explanation we need for our own understanding. Do you confess in your journal that you have "pedagogyaphobia," a debilitating neurosis grounded in being exposed to educational jargon invented by non-practicing educators who have completed the required years of psychoanalysis? I can't ask the questions about unseemly thoughts because that would not be politically correct. If you have a preoccupation in these areas, find a counselor immediately, especially if you seek to "get" those students who regularly make sport of you. Do you ask a lot of questions in your journal such as, Why did I accept this position and did I properly calculate how many years I need to put in before retirement? Are you a relationship-driven person who thinks that you can really change the thinking and performance of those constituents that just don't get it? (Of course, you may need mirrors for such a performance.) Do you reflect on the countless hours and energy spent on issues that could be resolved with a five-minute phone call to the right person? Nobody is going to own me, you say? Why the guilt entry on rationalizing preferential treatment to the son of the school board member?

How about the "bite my tongue" entry where you hold your breath for days hoping that procedural mishaps and impropriety don't come back to your office with a lawyer-escorted parent contingent?

Ah, the journal is, in fact, cathartic and offers many opportunities to reflect, doesn't it? Writing notes to oneself can also have therapeutic benefits, as the journal is the "id" Freud spoke about. The principal, more than any other professional, must know how he "feels" on issues, since he is often surrounded by rigid, linear thinkers, especially on issues with which faculty and parents are concerned. Have you ever made the "What do they think I am, a baby sitter?" entry? Working with teachers with fragile egos and low self-esteem is much more difficult than dealing with oppositional students, custodians, librarians, and superintendents all together. How about the teacher who tells his classes that he thinks he was abducted by aliens? How do you explain that to parents? We do in fact work in a profession with more than its share of eccentrics. With time, educators who were odd to begin with will become more dysfunctional and require as much attention as two-year-old children. If you have more than four or five of these on your staff, then you should probably think about hiring a personal psychotherapist—if you don't already have one.

Another great thing about journals lies in the fact that you can jump from one topic to the next without having to think about coherence. Did you forget Secretary's Day or, even worse, your secretary's birthday? Burn in a figurative hell for that one, baby, and don't even think about crying in your journal about it.

Read back your entries frequently and try to be objective about whether or not you sound like you're complaining, stressed out, frustrated, or misunderstood. If this is the case, it's time to change perspective or jobs, because the cold reality is that nobody really cares. Accept this as gospel and you, too, may remove the shackles of self-imposed martyrdom.

CHAPTER 4

Climate-Focused Leaders: The Profile

Read all the theory you want, attend seminars, conferences, conventions and forums, hire consultants, psychoanalysts, personal trainers, exorcists, or perhaps sponsor a séance to resurrect the spirit of John Dewey. Invite Bob Dylan to sing "The Times They Are a-Changing" or confront your mortality as a principal through Robert Frost's "The Road Not Taken."

You can do all these things and more while continuing to sink deeper into the role of the victim. As more educational leaders are steamrollered by big business' educational reform initiatives, they become more conservative, disillusioned, and downright paranoid, while losing sight of what they need to do as managers of a complex bureaucratic organization. Invariably, these leaders lose their perspective, becoming reactive instead of proactive and eventually losing their psychological edge.

The road to developing the climate-focused learning style begins with what Abraham Maslow called self-actualization. A hard look within is all it takes. It's a matter of becoming introspective about oneself in a leadership role while making self-improvements, rather than looking to change the system and others. If you think you're going to change the system first while putting yourself on the back burner, you can expect to be frustrated, overwhelmed, stressed out, and eventually burned out.

Climate-focused leaders do not work to survive; they don't complain about the system, or whine about directives or the school board's policies. They don't succumb to the "stuff flows down" continuum while driving their staffs into educational schizophrenia each time the central office imposes initiative two before initiative one is completed. They don't waste their time on those things that are beyond their control and, by being introspective, they know what those things are. These leaders like the "juice," the spontaneity of the day, along with the challenge of helping students, faculty, and parents solve problems. They are crafty mediators and enthusiastic motivators of people.

More importantly, these leaders are masters at delegating authority and empowering staff people to use their professional skills to get things done independently of them. They always know how to "work the crowd," but they are never insincere. Their constituents draw on their energy, vision, autonomy, and values. It goes without saying that these leaders are good role models for their employees. By demonstrating with consistency what they want done, climate-focused leaders make faculty and staff understand that everyone must be accountable for enforcing policies, following procedures, and holding true to the mission of the school.

Curriculum reform, professional development, high-stakes testing analysis, communications, public relations, supervision and evaluation, and so on will continue to remain stagnant, contrived, and unfinished until the school climate and culture are synchronized. This breed of leaders demonstrate through their own actions that until the culture and climate in the building are right, the school will not grow or evolve.

The fearless climate-driven administrator is a hands-on individual, who places his trust in those to whom he delegates authority. When his constituents fail, he inspires them to pick up the pieces and start over. More importantly, when his associates have success, he insists that they celebrate their successes while never stealing their thunder or taking bows for their efforts. He challenges his faculty to take risks in going the extra mile for students. He wins the respect of the staff by taking a clear stand on the make-or-break issues. Many of those issues involve the consistent administration of discipline, regardless of whether or not the students involved are the children of prominent members of the community. These leaders take on parents in support of good teachers when necessary, while making it clear to those teachers who are out of line that they must remain accountable and dignified when parents come in to take them apart.

Climate-focused school leaders are visionaries who accept responsibility for their actions while clearly articulating their values to all constituents. They never talk "Zen" or keep people guessing. Faculty and staff always know where they stand on issues because their actions mirror their convictions. More importantly, they work at developing a loyal following and always keep more informed about their enemies than their friends. By doing this, they avoid the costly and time-consuming pitfalls of "political suicide." Like poker players, they never chase cards or get in a game with strange players, and take calculated risks and raise the stakes only when they have a winning hand.

Probably the most important thing a climate-oriented school leader does is to get each and every member of the school community invested. This includes administrators, teachers, staff, students, and parents. This is no easy task, and can be realized only when the leader is willing to relinquish control by trusting and empowering his constituents to be active contributors in reform initiatives. It goes without saying that he must be a good listener.

When school leaders become overwhelmed by the number of things they have to deal with in the course of a day and in a school year, they become anxious, stressed, and vulnerable. As their resistance is compromised, the likelihood of making bad decisions by becoming reactive instead of proactive increases. This self-imposed pressure results from his inability to delegate enough responsibility and neglecting to invest the time necessary to teach people how to handle that responsibility. Dictatorial leaders have the shortest life in any organization, especially in education, where building relationships based on loyalty and trust is essential to both survival and productivity.

Organizational skills and the ability to juggle balls is a make-or-break factor for the climate-oriented leader. His ability to fend off the inclination to become preoccupied with a single issue while remaining focused on the big picture is essential to the efficient day-to-day operation of the organization. Enlisting the advice and expertise of specialists in matters in which he is not well versed gives him the assurance that he will never be unprepared to answer questions on any issues related to his authority.

Changing the culture in his organization will weigh heavily on his interpersonal skills. His credibility from day one will be established through his ability to communicate with people in a manner ensuring that they will be clear on what's being said. More importantly, he must do what he says will be done, and have the humility to admit to any wrongdoings or mistakes. Needless to say, he must model through personal actions what is expected of others. In demanding that the climate in the building ensure that each and every individual treats others with respect and dignity, he can never be excused for violating this doctrine by losing control with others.

Additionally, these leaders have the uncanny ability to win people over by boosting their confidence and self-worth. They do this by seizing every possible opportunity to pay compliments to others for jobs well done. The likelihood of desired behavior occurring with more regularity is enhanced by the constant reinforcement of good behavior. This well-documented Skinnerian principle does wonders in minimizing negative situations.

The climate-oriented school administrator lives and dies by the belief that people, not programs, drive school improvement. His approach to meeting the demands of high-stakes testing will be focused on the responsibility of teachers, students, and parents alike. Test scores and data will not be used to minimize the quality of performance but to serve as the basis for changing curriculum, attitudes, and behavior to bring about improvement. There will be no place for the "who's to blame" continuum in this leader's organization as all energies will be directed to solutions brought about through collaboration. Programs outside of the core areas will not be unnecessarily compromised or sacrificed to make room for remediation initiatives. The specific needs of individual students will be addressed, rather than a generalized picture of the entire student body. By enlisting the services of team leaders, setting realistic goals, and arming teachers with the needed tools for improvement, the school improvement plan has integrity and meaning.

Finally, public relations initiatives that are deliberate, informative, and well timed are critical in winning community support for climate-based school reform. By gaining the approval of the community, the school leader spends less time with disgruntled parents who, when knowing they are a distinct minority, usually remain silent. By returning all phone calls and responding to every reasonable concern raised by parents and others in the community, these leaders gain respect by showing respect. Visibility, not only in the school, but also at athletic contests, fundraisers, concerts, and other town-wide events gives these leaders a needed edge in maintaining the support of the public.

Take a moment to take the short quiz at the end of the chapter to determine whether or not you are a climate-focused administrator.

ARE YOU A CLIMATE FOCUSED ADMINISTRATOR?

This checklist is designed to help you reflect on your leadership style as it relates to enhancing school climate by developing a school culture where all members of the school community are invested.

_____ 1. Are you part of a high-performance administrative team where each member of the team has well-defined responsibilities?

_____ 2. Do you delegate authority unconditionally?

_____ 3. Do teachers follow the chain of command and generally perform their duties well?

_____ 4. Do you consistently praise and compliment teachers for jobs well done?

_____ 5. Are teachers who act unprofessionally or fail to perform their duties properly disciplined in a progressive manner?

_____ 6. Are teachers who are having problems in the classroom observed frequently and placed on regularly monitored improvement plans?

_____ 7. Are members of the support staff held to lofty but reasonable standards in situations where keeping information confidential and dealing with teachers, students, and parents are concerned?

_____ 8. Are staff members valued and frequently reminded how important they are to the school community?

_____ 9. Are students invested in the school? Are they given a voice in reform initiatives that directly impact them?

_____ 10. Do students show trust and confidence in their teachers and administrators?

_____ 11. Do students feel safe in the school?

_____ 12. Do students feel they are treated fairly and consistently? Do they understand the handbook and how they are expected to behave in the school building and at all cocurricular activities?

____ 13. Is discipline administered for the purpose of deterring undesirable behavior rather than as punishment?

____ 14. Do department heads and team leaders share teacher observation responsibilities with the administration?

____ 15. Do you have a Principal's Advisory Committee that is active in representing the faculty in school reform initiatives?

____ 16. Do you have a student Peer Mediation Program that is well developed and helps in the escalation and prevention of student-to-student conflict?

____ 17. Do you sponsor a Mentor Teacher Program where veteran faculty members spend time coaching and helping new teachers adjust and perform their jobs?

____ 18. Do teachers regularly engage in professional growth activities?

____ 19. Do you hold full faculty meetings only when necessary and not because there is a regular schedule to keep?

____ 20. Do teachers have an opportunity to evaluate administrators? Do students evaluate faculty?

____ 21. Are students invested and given a voice in school reform initiatives?

____ 22. Is your school building clean and orderly?

____ 23. Do the people on your faculty and staff have a good sense of humor? Do they laugh a lot and enjoy working with young people?

____ 24. Are social functions and appreciation gestures regularly offered to school workers?

____ 25. Are teachers accountable for student learning while making students more accountable for their own learning?

CHAPTER 5

The Guiding Principles of Success

There are no preparatory programs that can ready a school administrator for the numerous unforeseen situations that will occur at the worst possible times and have no obvious solutions. Successful professionals, regardless of their field of work, share the same defining qualities and expectations. To begin with, they are intuitive about people, they know their limitations, and they always play to win. These same professionals are leaders of others, are not afraid to take risks, thrive upon pressure, and never compromise their values. Additionally, they expect nothing but the best from themselves and their colleagues, they will never be outworked, and they are always prepared, even when they are unprepared.

One might ask how it is possible to prepare for what is both unforeseen and unexpected. The answer lies in one's ability to develop and live by the fundamental principles and laws that govern one's profession.

It is especially important for school administrators to establish some guiding principles based on the realities of the job. A handful of those basic beliefs, much like "Murphy's Laws," can become effective coping strategies in themselves.

A number of years as a school administrator and numerous discussions with many of my colleagues have helped me to construct a list of basic guiding principles that have served me well.

BRUCATO'S LAWS

1. Place the best interests of the students in your school above all else and your most difficult decisions will become less difficult.

2. If you need to make everybody happy in order to feel successful, get the hell out of school administration as fast as you can.

3. You will be defined by your ability to make the tough call. Blow one or two and you may find yourself on the second team.

4. Giving in to political pressure is like selling your soul to the devil.

5. Effective administrators are like "Vulcans." They function on logic, not emotion.

6. Never let angry parents rent space in your head.

7. Only two kinds of school administrators fail to use their annual allotment of personal and vacation days, the ones who are martyrs or damn fools.

8. When you start to spend more time at school and less time with family and friends, you have lost your perspective.

9. If you want to take the stress out of the job, start laughing at things, including yourself!

10. Make an enemy of your staff and coworkers and you have made an enemy of yourself.

11. You can only be successful by surrounding yourself with successful people.

12. State boards of education are like Santa Claus, the tooth fairy, and the Easter bunny; once you become older and wiser, you realize that they can't deliver what they promise.

13. If you have concluded that the best benefit of becoming a school administrator is in the retirement package, then you have, in fact, become self-actualized.

14. If you want to discover a potentially outstanding young teacher, find a prospective candidate who has a background in team sports.

15. Longevity in educational leadership can be attributed to one of two things: one's ability to think like Peter Pan or having a vast knowledge of existentialism or yoga.

16. As soon as you start thinking that you can't be replaced, you have one foot out the door.

17. You have sold out on your students when you stop your pursuit of the termination of a poor teacher.

18. Beware of those educational leaders who talk about team building when they've never lined up to play.

19. Your ability to lead can only be determined by those who will trust and follow you.
20. Your work ethic is only as good as your intentions.
21. When the threat of litigation influences what you do, you have defined yourself as a leader motivated by fear.

CHAPTER 6

Building an Administrative Team: The Foundation of a Well-Run School

Team builders are team players who know that their success will be contingent upon the success and effectiveness of their assistants and coworkers. Team builders are also experienced advocates who have defended controversial ideas, overcome adverse conditions, and willingly subordinated personal gain to the betterment of the team.

Building an effective administrative team for a school is no different than doing the same for a business, industry, or athletic program. The same principles are applicable and the cardinal rules remain unchanged.

As a prerequisite, team leaders must be individuals with a solid sense of self, thoroughly committed to leading by example. Unwavering in character and conviction, these strong people accept responsibility for their actions, demand loyalty and trust of their constituents, and always give the same in return.

- Team builders are motivators. They can readily assess strengths and weaknesses and have the charismatic ability to get their people to perform beyond their potential.
- Team builders have little use for control and have no use for dominance. Therefore, they do not dictate to others or accept credit for accomplishments.
- They rarely use "I." "We" is dominant in their everyday vocabulary.
- A team builder is demanding but will never ask of others what he will not do.
- Going the extra mile is a nonnegotiable expectation, as is doing whatever amount of work is necessary to get the job done.

- In return for their dedication to the team, the leader gives his lieutenants the autonomy to do their jobs, thus empowering them to assume key responsibilities in the leadership.

All of these principles must be applied and demonstrated through specific actions of the leader if team members are to fall into line.

THE SICILIAN MODEL

Although its goals are vastly different, I refer to my team-building strategy as the "Sicilian Model" because all members of the leadership team must be devoted to one another, never betraying trust or publicly displaying disloyalty. They must put "family" (the team) first, and always be prepared to come to the defense of their colleagues whenever there is a need. All disputes are resolved within the team, during the formation of a position. (There can be occasions, then, when an individual cannot continue as a team member due to irreconcilable differences with team direction or a team decision.)

This is, also, very much the American way. As I recall, the very same principles of team building were effectively employed when our Revolutionary Army defeated a superior British war machine to win us our independence. It is significant to note, in this respect, that even George Washington had his dissenters, who, like Benedict Arnold, and, to a lesser extent, Horatio Gates, had to leave the team.

Unfortunately, most people stereotypically weld the Sicilian tradition to the "Godfather Trilogy," which sensationalized and rationalized murder as an acceptable means of handling disloyal family members. Thus, "Sicilian" has become synonymous with Mafia and Cosa Nostra which is as much a falsehood as any other stereotype. The fact of the matter is, the Sicilians are a proud, family-centered people who love life and know how to separate work from play. More importantly, they raise their children to respect their elders, family, and culture while never behaving in ways that will degrade themselves or disgrace the family. This aspect of the Sicilian culture indicates what feelings provide the philosophical bonding for a strong team.

Most educators to whom I have spoken over the years seem to agree that, it is more than anything else, the lack of respect for authority and the tendency for young people to be egocentric that has made our jobs difficult, and in some cases, impossible. I am no more of an idealist than the next educator, but I do believe that it is our primary responsibility to teach young people and fellow educators that character education goes hand in hand with academic instruction. The very knowledge that we seek to impart becomes less valuable in the absence of good character in its possessors.

When I began my tenure as my school's principal, five years ago, I was determined to remain devoted to the cause of making the school a better institution by staying focused on the cultural issues that affected the climate of the building. With the seemingly impossible workload and no assistants in place, I knew there was only one way to stay the course; I needed people who would willingly share with me the responsibilities, while working in the best interest of the team.

I had to build a team.

It would be difficult to identify one quality assistant, let alone two, and my experience as a vice-principal would have to suffice in putting both assistants in place prior to opening school. As a further complication, I had only three weeks to get this done.

The application pool wasn't exactly saturated with candidates and I would not take any chances on hiring people about whom I had no knowledge and whom I could not personally endorse. Fortunately, I had in the school two colleagues with excellent reputations in the school community who were willing to jump into the fire. Their lack of experience in the role did not concern me as they were outstanding teachers with a proven work ethic. Having ready-made credibility with students and faculty as well as a strong knowledge of the school, my assistants-to-be had only the need to decide if they were ready for the biggest professional challenge of their lives. In terms of personal qualities, Dennis and John had all of the essentials, even though they were two very different individuals. Both had extensive teaching, coaching, and extracurricular advising experience, coupled with intelligence and the willingness to learn. I was confident I had a pair of potential administrative winners. Additionally, both men were perceived in the school as individuals of strong character who would be able to work effectively with oppositional students.

In building my team, then, I followed the precept of valuing character and potential over experience. I have had no cause to regret this decision.

When building a leadership team, it is better, I think, to select individuals based on personal qualities rather than experience in the role. It is also worthy of note that managing a faculty is a much different and more difficult task than managing students. Teachers have a much different view of former teachers in administrative roles. In fact, most teachers who have been around for awhile will not give an administrator who hasn't been in the "trenches" the time of day. Therefore, I feel that well-chosen former teachers with achieved faculty credibility have an edge when moving into the role.

The job of school leaders today is one that is learned while in the role. There are no methods courses for school leadership that can realistically simulate the environment in which administrators live and function. You won't find a "how-to" manual and you can be guaranteed that no two days will be the same or that what worked for one situation will work for another.

I learned early on that even though our school handbooks are written in black and white, we forever live in the gray. There are no two people exactly alike; how can we possibly think we can find the same amicable resolution for similar situations? Team members must share this realization and be prepared to deal with multiple problems and individual solutions.

Due to the ineffectiveness of attempts to generalize and duplicate the same approaches to the same problems involving different people, intuition can easily be the leader's greatest strength. Those aspiring administrators, no matter how well they are formally trained, who don't have a genuine love of people, and the stomach for a steady diet of conflict and controversy, will have unpleasant and, usually, unsuccessful tenures. Nonconfrontational individuals without thick skin and a strong sense of self, will certainly not enjoy, let alone survive, the job of a school leader.

Teaching experienced teachers the job of assistant principal is much easier, it seems to me, than mentoring an already-experienced administrator, as the teacher has no preconceived notions or convictions about how things should be done. I would proceed to teach my two new assistants their jobs from my firsthand experience and what I knew of the experience of others in the position. This case-oriented, school-specific, anecdotal approach is what inspires my writing, since it is such a far cry from the clinical methods that, for me, have kept missing the mark. I also write because the current shortage of administrative candidates makes the selection of inside personnel much more attractive than it has traditionally been, thus supporting what is a general viewpoint of mine.

With five years in the role of assistant principal and another two as a dean of students, I have many stories to tell. Each story has a moral and the most important ones embody a lesson, which has value in how not to act, respond, or proceed. From these lessons or tips on "How Not to Fall on the Sword," I fashioned my "Key Responsibility Areas" which would serve as the twenty commandments of my climate-focused administrative team.

KRAS (KEY RESPONSIBILITY AREAS) FOR ADMINISTRATORS

1. Be fair, firm, honest, and consistent with students, faculty, and parents.
2. Be proactive instead of reactive.
3. Document, document, document (all situations and interactions should be written and filed).
4. Be clear in your expectations with both students and teachers. Communicate and test for understanding.
5. Get out of your office and into the hallways and classrooms; be visible.
6. Do more drop-by or informal observations than formal observations—follow up where needed.
7. When unclear about a law, policy, process, or procedure, get direction before acting.
8. Demand that you get an accurate attendance report from teachers each and every day—no exceptions. Follow up on *all* errors.
9. Never discuss students with students or teachers with teachers; maintain confidentiality at all times.
10. Never discipline a student when you are angry or emotional. Revisit the situation when you are not emotional.
11. Do not give teachers a nonproductive "pound of flesh" where disciplining students is concerned. Insist that they become part of the solution or resolution.

12. Keep your door open to student, teachers, and parents. Listen! Listen! Listen!

13. Never discipline a student for a *second* time without contacting a parent! If it is a serious matter (fighting, drugs, alcohol, harassment, theft, vandalism, etc.), contact parents immediately.

14. Accentuate the positive! Hand out deserved compliments, accolades, and acknowledgments in abundance. Send complimentary notes whenever merited to both students and teachers.

15. If you have to speak to a teacher a second time about not fulfilling duties and/or responsibilities, send a memo of concern (always send a copy to fellow administrators). If a third violation should occur, set up a meeting with the principal, yourself, and the teacher or staff member without delay.

16. Harassment and vulgarity will not be tolerated and should be treated as the most serious offenses that you deal with. Follow procedures to the letter.

17. Keep a daily log of all individuals with whom you deal—students, parents, teachers, or staff—and document the interactions (need not be formal).

18. Never violate the trust and integrity of the administrative team. We are *one*. Some people will consistently try to drive wedges or play one of us against another. This can't happen! Loyalty must be maintained at all times!

19. Never put your hands on a student for any reason. Also, refrain from calling names or making hasty value judgments, as they will come back to haunt you.

20. Make your secretary your best friend and confidante. Make sure she knows exactly what you expect and listen to her recommendations. Elevate her from secretary to office manager. Ask her to make decisions and help you with information. Never forget Secretary's Day or her birthday.

The most influential educational consultant I ever had the privilege of working with was a gentleman by the name of Don Craig, whom I met while working as a dean of students at an independent school in Miami, Florida. Don was emphatic in pointing out that responsibilities are often miscommunicated, inferred, or simply not made clear to employees by their superiors. When subordinates are not schooled in the specifics of each and every duty they are expected to perform, chances are, the boss is spending most of his time cleaning up messes and doing damage control.

Don would always ask us "Did you do your Key Responsibility Areas (KRAs)?" prior to discussing problematic situations related to school personnel because he felt that problems could be clearly identified as long as the individuals involved know exactly what is expected of them. The KRAs should be clearly written, copied, and visited often for assessment of job performance, as well as self-reflection.

When the administrative team-building process begins, KRAs must first be established and discussed before specific duties requiring supervision of others by a team member are delegated. KRAs do not represent overall goals but desired behaviors for which all members of the team must be accountable. KRAs, therefore, become the basis for maintaining consistency and holding the team together.

KRAs also provide team members with some clear-cut ground rules that can be used to measure personal successes and growth. I am careful in not dwelling on "goals" or holding my assistants accountable for them. The KRAs, unlike goals, can be achieved through one's personal commitment without the involvement of others. Also, unlike goals, KRAs are objectives that must be achieved regularly if the team is to meet with success.

The only major goal-like precept that I established for my leadership team is one that more or less takes care of itself if the KRAs are properly fulfilled. The goal emphasizes the necessity for problem solving at the lowest-possible level. The goal very simply states:

> It is the job of the assistant principal to do everything in his power to keep matters from reaching the principal's desk and it is the job of the principal to prevent things from getting to the superintendent.

For me, that says it all.

BREAKDOWN OF RESPONSIBILITIES

School leaders constantly complain about having too many responsibilities and too little time to get everything done. This is a legitimate complaint if there is, in fact, only one administrator to run the school. It is more than likely, though, that the leader hasn't done enough in delegating responsibilities to assistants, department heads, directors, and curriculum team leaders.

Administrators are no different than teachers in that they learn by doing. The more opportunities inexperienced administrators have to learn the multiple tasks of the job, the more quickly they will become acclimated and capable of doing an increasing number of things. One thing is certain: if the school leader, be it a principal or superintendent, does not place his trust in the members of the administrative team by sharing the responsibilities, the assistants will forever be robbed of critical learning experiences, and the team will bog down. Micromanaging is the nemesis of team building!

Team builders relish every opportunity to teach their assistants how to run a school and empower them to do so by giving them specific duties to perform. When assistants know that they have the support and confidence of their superior, who is willing to be patient, while enjoying the role of mentor, they will willingly take on additional duties. Once the school leader makes clear the chain of command and insists that school personnel adhere to it, those multiple interruptions that can occur on a daily basis will decrease, since more than one administrator will be available to handle issues that arise.

After making clear to my assistants what their key responsibilities were, I was ready to assign each of them specific responsibilities. When you have two or more assistants, you obviously have very different individuals with ready-made strengths and skills to help you decide who should be assigned what duty. Having listed all of the major responsibilities of the administration, I was ready to assign the assistants accordingly. We were working with a two-house system in which each assistant was responsible for monitoring approximately six hundred students.

Responsibilities

Principal

Prepare and Manage Budget
Capital Improvement
Supervise Department Heads and Directors

Assess School Data
Professional Development
District Administrative Team
Community Relations
Chair School Council
Newspaper Television
Attend School Committee Meetings
Hire, Evaluate, Dismiss, Discipline Underperforming School Personel

Assistant Principals

Discipline Students
Observe/Supervise Faculty
Supervise Hall and Security Monitors
Chaperone Dances, Proms, Cocurricular Activities
Work with Counselors, Youth Officers, Courts, Dept. of Social Services, Dept. of Youth Services
Schedule and Supervise Substitute Teachers

ASSISTANT 1
Student Activities Coordinator
Special Education Liaison
ESL/Bilingual Liaison
Student/Parent Handbook
   Committee Chair
Senior Awards Program
Senior Night Program
Graduation Program
Character Education
Boys State/Girls State, Daughters
   of the American Revolution
Mentor Teacher Program
Building Aesthetics
Severe Needs Program Liaison
Supervise Peer Leadership
   Program
Tobacco Education
Video Surveillance

ASSISTANT 2
Academic Schedule
Activity Academic Calendar
Student/Faculty Parking
Lockers/Keys; Security
Athletics, Sports Awards Liaison
Community Liaison; Attend
Functions in Absence of Principal
Custodians, Facilities Liaison
Activity Day, Exams
Video Production Supervisor
Mass. Comprehensive Assessment
   System Delivery System/
   Statistical
Analysis (State-Mandated Testing)
Teacher Grading/Report Cards
Special Schedules
Curriculum/District/Assessment
   Team Liaison

One administrator should be at all tournament games, where possible.
One administrator should be at all dances.
One administrator should be at all proms.

The most important thing that I did for my assistants was to allow them to develop mastery of at least one critical area of our administration. By doing this, I was freeing up time for myself while developing a "master" on my team, who could both advise me and handle all administrative matters within that given area. My interests were not completely selfish, as I was helping to make my assistants more marketable as principals. Furthermore, I was helping them establish their identity in the school as educational leaders and supported decision makers.

I'm sure you would agree that developing the master schedule is an arduous task that is always time-consuming and never goes as planned. It is especially difficult to develop a semester block, 4×4 schedule for 1,150 students. With a new software program in place and a school year of training ahead, I gave this task to my first assistant, Dennis, who would work tirelessly with my director of guidance to learn and master the system. Dennis, a former physical education teacher and football coach with limited knowledge of technology, would soon become our scheduling guru. Two years later, he became the principal of a neighboring high school, in part because of his mastery of scheduling and the unique leadership style he cultivated while working independently of me. I considered this a success of the team concept, even though I lost a valuable subordinate.

Since Dennis was absorbed with the scheduling process, John would take on the role of director of cocurricular activities. He was a natural, having done many years as a class advisor. His background as a mathematics teacher gave him the needed edge in organizing and administering our numerous activity programs. After one year in the role, John decided to return to the classroom but not because he didn't do an outstanding job in the role. A steady diet of student discipline, which is an ever-present reality of the job, was of little interest to John who made a personal decision that I respected and supported. *It is another strength of the team that it so clearly defines what is necessary that such decisions can be made more soundly.*

Dennis and John paved the way for their successors, Nancy and Rick, who have been equally autonomous and eager to move from master teachers to master administrators. I have been fortunate to have such outstanding assistants; it is important to note, however, that I have been as devoted to them as they have been to me. I am still, as an administrator, in a teaching role, and therefore have been dedicated to mentoring my assistants. I thoroughly enjoy this role, but more importantly, I believe that this is what all school leaders must do if they want to build an effective and smoothly functioning team. In addition to their critical area, my assistants would:

- manage their individual offices,
- handle all matters related to student affairs, including discipline and extracurricular functions,
- split the responsibilities related to screening and supervising substitute teachers,
- manage hall monitors,
- complete a number of teacher observations.

This would give me additional time that would allow me to work more closely with department heads and directors who would be included as part of the leadership team. By giving more authority to these individuals to manage the people in their departments, I am further delegating administrative responsibilities.

Both my assistants and department heads would be trained in the formal observation process and their observations would be the foundation of my evaluations.

I did not accept the point of view that department heads and directors could not be considered supervising administrators, since they were in the same union as their colleagues. They were, after all, teaching fewer sections and had a very specific and detailed job description, which included numerous supervisory duties. I needed their help in the following: supervising the teaching staff, especially where mentoring young and inexperienced teachers was concerned; playing a major role in hiring new teachers, as each department head would be asked to thoroughly interview candidates whenever an opening in their department occurred; and those other routine, standard book-stamping, budget-keeping responsibilities that have so often reduced valuable leadership team personnel to clerical staff.

DEPARTMENT HEAD RESPONSIBILITIES

Managerial Components

Department Heads will:

1. Conduct and supervise all department meetings including the required monthly meeting.
2. Channel information to members of their department.
3. Develop and maintain a professional library.
4. Represent their department at meetings involving curriculum co-ordination.
5. Develop and manage the department budget (books, supplies, equipment, etc.) and the disbursement of such throughout the school year. Initiate purchase orders and follow-up receipt of same. Maintain inventory of supplies and books.
6. Attend monthly administrative meetings and other administrative/staff meetings as necessary.
7. Coordinate student teaching assignments within the department.

Curriculum Development

Department Heads will:

1. Work with department teachers in constructing and developing/revising objectives, activities, and evaluation designs.
2. Work cooperatively with other department chairs in developing integration and correlation between various teaching areas.
3. Work with teachers in developing/revising and evaluating curriculum and selection of textbooks.
4. Solicit input from department staff regarding course assignments. Forward and work with administration and guidance on teacher assignments.

5. Develop and maintain an extensive ancillary library available to teachers to augment activities within their course.
6. Apply the strands and objectives, as specified in the Curriculum Frameworks and Virginia Plan, to the current curriculum and monitor their use in each teacher's classroom.
7. Encourage team sharing, peer teaching, inter and intradepartmental cooperation.
8. Conduct departmental meetings discussing Curriculum-Scope and Sequence.
9. Encourage teachers to use various teaching/learning styles.
10. Coordinate meetings with middle and high school staff to discuss curriculum concerns.

Curriculum Supervision and Assessments

Department Heads will:

1. Supervise the performance of staff and make recommendations to improve teaching performances. The principal will take the department head's observation under advisement before he makes a recommendation for continuation and/or retention of staff.
2. Supervise and assist substitute teachers (making sure materials and assignments are clear to substitute).
3. Develop and implement a procedure that enables teachers to observe and discuss the progress of others teaching the same curriculum.
4. Coordinate time for the development or revision of departmentalized exams that are used to evaluate and review curriculum and its implementation.
5. Recommend teaching assignments based upon teacher strengths for the best possible curriculum implementation.
6. Ensure that lesson plans are left for substitute and check regularly on the decorum of a substitute's class.
7. Keep morale positive by listening attentively to teacher problems and arbitrate disputes objectively.

8. Demonstrate effective teaching strategies and encourage teachers to share materials and strategies.
9. Make assessments on teacher's performance.

Program Evaluations

Department Heads will:

1. Assess standardized test scores and make curriculum adjustments where applicable, i.e., PSAT scores, SAT scores, AP examination scores, MCAS results, etc.
2. Stress a variety of styles such as alternative assessment methods (portfolios, contracts, etc.), open-ended questions, community-oriented projects, multimedia, computer-related education, and student-centered learning styles and critical thinking.
3. Conduct follow-up studies of graduates.
4. Conduct individual conferences with teachers.

Personnel Supervision and Evaluation

Department Heads will:

1. Supervise and observe department staff and provide observation reports to help enhance teaching performance.
2. Be visible in the hallways as much as possible to keep teachers at their posts and to help reduce student infractions between classes.
3. Monitor teacher absenteeism and encourage teachers to maintain good attendance.
4. Conduct meetings with teachers to delineate what they feel they need to strengthen their skills.

SUPERVISION AND OBSERVATION

Each member of the leadership team must have an active role in the supervision of school personnel as well as the formal observation of teachers. Regardless of the size of the faculty and staff, it is imperative that a number of individuals are identified as authority figures to whom staff must answer. If done properly and consistently, this shared responsibility can have a major impact on the climate of a school, especially where the nonconformist members of the faculty who may not, historically, have been held accountable are concerned. The supervising administrator needs first to be a good role model for others by adhering to every policy and expectation he is asked to oversee. This is the only way in which the administrator will gain the credibility essential for his effectiveness.

If teachers are not properly supervised, you can be sure that many of them are not doing their job in supervising students. When this is the case, discipline becomes centralized. Even small matters will require handling by assistant principals, deans, and house masters, who will be spending an inordinate amount of time on student discipline. I constantly remind my assistants that if they spend more time supervising and working with teachers, especially those who are weak disciplinarians, they will spend less time on student discipline.

The formal observation process is equally important and much more complex. Different school systems adhere to various observation models, but the goal of creating a meaningful opportunity for teachers to become reflective while improving in their methodology remains the same. Whatever the model, a training component is essential for the observers to make it work. We can assume that a former teacher having notoriety as an excellent instructor can recognize good teaching. What we can't count on, however, is if the same individual as an observer can get beyond the defenses of those they observe in order to make a difference. Making a difference involves the ability to identify what needs to be improved and make a valid recommendation on how to improve it.

Hiring a consultant to help administrators write observation reports, conduct pre- and post-conference interviews, and compare scripts is helpful, but mastering the psychology of the process is far more important. Teachers are actors who love the stage. This is especially true of veteran educators who can turn a mediocre lesson into a winner, even when caught off guard. Therefore, winning the psychological edge begins in part with a very specific focus on what is being observed as well as what constitutes good teaching. For the observation process to have any utility at all, subjectivity has to be removed, as far as possible, from the operation.

Most administrators will have advanced knowledge of content in one or two areas at best; therefore, the content of a lesson should not usually be the focus of an observation. If content is a problem, expertise will have to be obtained as provided in the law. In nearly all cases, observers need only reflect on preestablished fundamental principles of effective teaching in all curricular areas. My teachers and observers alike are constantly reminded of these principles which are frequently revisited and reviewed.

MILFORD HIGH SCHOOL CLASSROOM INSTRUCTION— ALL CURRICULAR AREAS

1. Standard Based—Curriculum Frameworks, Milford High School Curriculum
2. Focused Objective(s)—For each and every lesson—objective specifically related to standard
3. Active Learning—Continued expansion of methods geared at independent, student-directed learning.
4. Brisk pacing/multiple teaching methods
5. Authentic assessment
6. Raise expectations/accountability/accommodate learning styles
7. Expanded practice related to open-ended questions, critical thinking, and critical writing
8. Consistency
9. Record keeping
10. Preparation

Next, there must be some very specific procedures that are followed and they must be done in sequence. Without giving the process integrity, you can rest assured that both teachers and observers alike will go through the motions without any expectation of substantial results. The procedures should be clear cut and leave little room for improvisation. Observers with little or no experience are especially in need of a process that is applicable to every observation they will make.

OBSERVATION PROCESS

PC = Pre-Conference, AN = Announced, UN =Unannounced, Σ = Written Evaluation, N = New Teacher

All observations should be based upon the principles of effective teaching as well as the guidelines established for all teachers in all curricular areas.

Procedure

1. Have teacher complete Pre-Observation Form—Establish date and time of observation.
2. Be on time or early for your observation.
3. Stay focused on the following:
   - Objective(s) —Does teacher stay focused on objective(s)?
   - Organization/Transition—Does teacher look prepared?
   - Classroom Decorum—Are students attentive, orderly?
   - Involvement—Are all students participating/engaged?
   - Brisk Pacing—Is class briskly paced?
   - Teaching Methods—What methods are used? Are multiple methods used, Specifically, Expository (lecture), Group (co-operative), Question & Answer, Discussion, Simulation, Multi-media, Class Presentations, Independent Practice, Evaluation, Authentic Assessment?
4. Observe 40–50 minutes of class minimum—keep track of time (transitions), participation, etc.
5. Post conference same day or next day—either prep mod or after school (20–30 minutes maximum).
   - Ask questions during post-conference rather than make judgments.
   - Make recommendations—based on good teaching.
   - Don't "nitpick"—stay focused on the "big picture."
   - Take notes during post-conference.
   - Identify key components you want to include in written observation.
6. Write Observation
   - Be specific (should read like a narrative). Use examples for every value judgment you make. Example: Mrs. Jones works

very hard to keep all students engaged. While I was in the class, she asked almost every student a question and 15 out of the 17 students actively participated.

- Make recommendations clear and concise and based on *specifics* of observation—do not generalize!
- Make commendations based on utilization of Extended Learning Time, focus on objectives, preparation, classroom order, knowledge of subject, passion for students, rapport with students, etc.

7. Proofread Report
   - Clean up report before you send it to the teacher for signature. When returned signed, you sign it and return copy for his files.
   - Always keep confidential.
   - Never talk to another teacher about someone else's observation.
   - Save time and energy by taking control, maximizing your ability to create a worthwhile process, while holding all individuals accountable.

TEAM MEMBERS AS EFFECTIVE OBSERVERS

1. Consider personalities and subject backgrounds when matching teachers with observers.
2. Establish specific observation criteria that are applicable to all disciplines.
3. Define specific objectives for observing both veteran and new instructors.
4. Preserve the integrity of the process by holding all observers accountable for following the established process.
5. Provide the necessary training for all observers.
6. Ensure that underperforming instructors are given specific improvement plans that are revisited annually.
7. Resolve to help underperforming teachers improve and begin the process to terminate when no improvement is evident.
8. Use the process to reward teachers for excellent performance.

You are undoubtedly frustrated with matters relating to teacher observation if the goal of your district is to meet contractual obligations by observing a large number of teachers over a too-short period. If this is the case, you are wasting a lot of effort that could be invested in many other worthy initiatives and necessary tasks.

AGENDA-DRIVEN MEETINGS

When an administrative team is built on a solid foundation, team members all have well-defined responsibilities that they need time to fulfill. Meetings are a "time-draining" component of most organizations often leading to unproductive time.

It has been my experience that many times meetings are held because there is a predetermined schedule, or because the individual holding the meeting has an inner need for an audience while he pontificates. When this is the case, those individuals required to attend become frustrated, resentful, and at times even hostile. A classic example of the "unmeeting" is a school's bimonthly faculty meeting or "gripe session" which is a great opportunity for those people to whom nobody listens to hear themselves talk. When cogent agendas, not pre-set schedules, drive meetings, these negative situations can readily be avoided.

I meet with my assistants on a need-to basis and hold bimonthly meetings with department heads and directors as long as we have an agenda to follow. Monthly faculty meetings, although scheduled on a provisional basis, are rarely held, as my meetings with department heads and directors set the agendas for individual department meetings where administrative expectations are made clear and smaller group discussions can take place.

Prior to all meetings, it is my expectation that the facilitator will get the agenda out to all participants well in advance. Most meetings, if properly run, should serve as forums for disseminating information and distributing specific assignments. When the meeting becomes a discussion group this is the point at which things can begin to go downhill. By encouraging educators to voice their concerns with administrators on a regular basis, there is less of a need for discussion groups or lengthy meetings that are unfruitful due to size and diffusion.

Time management is a defining quality of efficient administrative teams, whose team members learn quickly the value of agenda-driven meetings that are purposeful and action oriented. They also learn the benefits of making individuals who attend their meetings active participants. When we attend meetings where our active involvement is required, our tendency is to be better prepared, more invested, and attentive.

Teachers are especially appreciative of being subjected to fewer meetings, especially when they are informative, brief, and interactive. I find it necessary to list the elements of efficiently run, agenda-driven meetings, because as logical and obvious as it all seems, school leaders often forget to adhere to the guiding principles.

The Guiding Principles of Agenda-Driven Meetings

1. Develop and distribute the agenda to all constituents in advance.
2. Make constituents active participants.
3. Keep it short. (Try to set a time limit and stick to it.)
4. Do not facilitate gripe sessions. (Personal feelings should not be denied, but visited in other forums.)
5. Insist that constituents are attentive and respectful to the facilitator or speaker.
6. Be cautious of ambitious agendas. (Assign ad hoc committees to research comprehensive items that can be revisited later.)
7. Allow constituents to make recommendations for agenda items.
8. Recap meeting resolutions and decisions. (Distribute follow-up minutes/memorandums when necessary.)
9. Leave no loose ends.
10. Rotate the facilitator wherever possible. (Give different individuals an opportunity to run the meeting.)

WINNING SUPPORT THROUGH TEAM UNITY AND RESPECT

Just as leaders are defined by their ability to build a loyal following, effective leadership teams will prove themselves worthy through the consistent performance of team members. School administrators, as part of the same team, will be forever challenged to remain unified when parents, students, and faculty attempt to drive wedges between them.

These leaders will never adversely respond to questions or issues about their teammates and will not commiserate with malcontents who seek to draw them in. Personal differences among team members are taken up behind closed doors; as "dirty laundry," it is never publicly aired. "Good Cop, Bad Cop" is a valuable strategy often employed by team members who regularly capitalize on the strength of their partnership to keep it from being compromised.

Those individuals in the school community who chronically complain, or have a negative opinion on just about everything, can be effectively isolated by cohesive leadership teams who are willing to listen to concerns and frustrations only when potential solutions are offered. When offhand complaints of a personal nature continue to fall on deaf ears, the frequency of the complaints will greatly diminish. Simply put, when you take away the host, there is nothing left for the germ to feed on, thus causing the infection to dissipate.

Effective school leadership teams are successful in getting more teachers to do their jobs in a better and more effective way. When this occurs, climate in the school improves as students and parents have fewer problems with teachers to take to administrators.

Winning the support of the faculty and staff will be the most difficult and most important thing the leadership team will have to accomplish in moving the school forward. Faculty members, especially, will determine the fate of their leadership group, which they will either accept as allies or defy and obstruct as enemies. Teaching staffs that are top heavy in veterans will demand that their leaders treat them fairly while never maligning them to parents, students, or political convenience. Teachers young and old will look to their administration for strength and courage, but above all, they will demand respect. The successful school leader is conscious of this from the moment he begins to build his team.

Students, too, must feel that they have a voice in the school. If the leadership team is not approachable, many students will take matters into their own hands and cause unrest among the student body and faculty. Contrary to what many people think, students are, in fact, receptive to discipline as long as it is administered equitably. Therefore, it is not only possible for the leadership to run a tight ship and still have the support of the majority of the students, it is an absolute necessity! Mutual respect is as equally important for the students as it is for the faculty.

Parents and other members of the community are an excellent source of feedback on leadership team effectiveness. Parents want to be heard. If you avoid their phone calls or inquiries you can expect to be branded as unapproachable or out of touch. Parents will also demand that you keep their children safe in the building. Mishaps involving student injuries, physical or mental, can ruin the most effective administrations. The team, therefore, can never do too much in promoting school safety, and student behavior.

Team members must be well schooled in matters involving individual student rights and due process. Like good lawyers, they must review case law and identify precedents for every controversial issue with which they deal. It is not enough to rely on the procedures established in the school handbook, as crafty legal minds, retained and financed by determined parents, will often find loopholes. A simple procedural mishap involving a single student can devastate the strongest of teams. Like a cohesive legal team, administrative leaders must always work together on the tough cases to make sure all bases are covered, and that all members are on the same page. By keeping on their legal and organizational toes, effective teams better their odds of staying out of court, and if there is a court case, of winning.

Another significant evaluative criteria of team effectiveness involves the administration's ability to keep the school on course. The team will be scrutinized by students and parents each time a reform initiative that means substantial change in the school is introduced. Faculty members especially are intolerant of an "overflowing platter"—being subjected to a second major initiative prior to completing the first one. Teachers lose respect for their leaders whenever they feel the "stuff flows down" continuum is in effect. This stems from the perception that the building administrator is not proactive but merely a conduit.

(When I began teaching in the late 1970s, I was a member of a very feisty faculty. In those days, it seemed that a sense of humor was a requirement for all teachers. One of our elder statesmen, the Director of Art, would seize every possible opportunity to critique our administration. He was a clever artist, historian, and master of creating satirical cartoons. The cartoons were funny, poignant, and painfully truthful. One cartoon [see figure 6.1] in particular was a perfect example of how school leaders succumb to the pressure of politics and higher authority to stray off course.)

Figure 6.1.

When teachers feel they are forever being subjected to directives by members of the leadership who have either lost touch with, or have never been in the classroom, they will demonstrate their dissatisfaction through resistance, apathy, and/or a subpar performance. As soon as battle lines are drawn, and it's clearly a matter of "us versus them," the leadership might as well pack up their tents and vacate the premises. There can be no effective administrative team that makes enemies out of its faculty members. On the other hand, the team that works in harmony with their faculty almost always assumes responsibility for whatever goes wrong in the school.

My colleague, the art director, also did some creative writing. One of his most notable works accurately depicted the disposition of our faculty concerning bureaucratic public school administration. We were, in fact, divided, and the leadership had allowed this to take place. As a result, many different factions within our faculty were aligned with one of three different administrators, and the team integrity was fatally compromised.

Did you know that when it came time to answer for the disastrous "Charge of the Light Brigade" during the Crimean War in 1854, Lord Cardigan, the English general in command, was able to side-step the responsibility to a colonel? He, in turn, pointed to a captain who indicated that the fault rested with the courier lieutenant who had penned the order. Now the lieutenant, being a good buck-passer like the rest, put the blame on a poor lance corporal who simply happened to be in the tent during the time the lieutenant was writing out the order. The corporal couldn't find a private. The Inquiry Board accepted all excuses. The Officer Corps was saved from disgrace (as usual), and the "enlisted swine" was convicted and shipped off to rot in some military stockade.

Nice, eh? Fun to march around rubbing elbows with all the other bigwigs, but, unlike Harry Truman, avoid responsibility for any mess you've created.

Always keep a scapegoat at hand!

Now that reminds me of another situation. . . .
The college professsors, "professional" educators, and doctoral candidates "innovate" "meaningful" programs for the public schools . . .
   BUT THEY AREN'T IN THE CLASSROOM!

The Directors of State and Federal funding rubber stamp each program. . . .
   BUT THEY AREN'T IN THE CLASSROOM!!

The Legislators back up such programs with mandates. . . .
   BUT THEY AREN'T IN THE CLASSROOM!!!

The School Committees approve such programs. . . .
   BUT THEY AREN'T IN THE CLASSROOM!!!!

The Public School District Administrators order the implementation of such programs. . . .
   BUT THEY AREN'T IN THE CLASSROOM!!!!!

The parents and the community activists cry out for such pro-
grams. . . .
    AND THEY AREN'T IN THE CLASSROOM EITHER!!!!!!

BUT YOU ARE TO BLAME FOR THE MESS IN PUBLIC EDU-
CATION TODAY, "CORPORAL."

As has been said . . . "It's difficult to soar with the eagles when
you work around the turkeys."

Each administrator had his or her own agenda and all frequently
made their differences with one another public. The culture of our
school was defined through this obvious rift in the leadership. The climate, therefore, was forever tense and volatile. Once the leadership
team is broken up or if it never materializes at the outset, it is almost
inevitable that a very poor climate will exist.

There are some very specific things that leadership teams can do to
improve school climate by encouraging faculty, students, and parents to
take an active role in school improvement initiatives, working both independently and collectively with school leaders.

ESTABLISHING A LEADERSHIP ADVISORY COMMITTEE

An advisory committee composed of teachers who represent the many
different interests and curricular areas in the school can be a valuable
asset to principals and school leaders. In order to ensure that the committee is credible, members should *not* be handpicked by the leadership. Their agendas should evolve out of the interests of the faculty,
while the leadership gives the committee the autonomy to take an active role in the ongoing school reform process. When it is apparent to
all members of the faculty that their committee is, in fact, active and
valued by the leadership, more teachers will feel vested while using this
forum to voice interests and concerns.

My advisory committee meets regularly and independently of me.
Their chairperson keeps me apprised of their initiatives and gives me
committee recommendations for policy amendments, procedural varia-
tions, and so on. I will take the recommendation back to my leadership

team and make every effort to make the modification the committee seeks. By creating a committee that is "action" based and focused on "solutions," the leadership has, in effect, added another important contingent to the leadership team. (If such a recommendation cannot be acted upon, it is imperative that the faculty group receive an explanation as to why it is not feasible.)

Give Teachers the Opportunity to Formally Evaluate the Leadership

When you give members of the faculty and support staff an opportunity to evaluate the leadership team, you are demonstrating to them that you mean what you say, while further challenging them to become active participants in the growth of your school. Many leaders neglect to do this trust-building activity because they fear the truth or lack the self-confidence to deal with it.

My advisory committee researched and chose a suitable evaluation tool, surveyed the faculty, and tabulated the results before giving me the synopsis. I, in turn, thanked the faculty for their input and responded to their concerns.

When this activity was completed, teachers had an opportunity to evaluate my assistant principals and department heads, following the same procedure.

MEET REGULARLY WITH STUDENT LEADERS

By keeping student leaders informed, while insisting that they actively represent their fellow students in school matters, they too will become more invested in their school. Student leaders in our school are included in a number of different committees such as the Student/Parent Handbook, Senior Night, and School Service Committees. Administrators meet regularly with the Student Leadership Council. The door is kept open between us, so that the students may ask for our input, or we may ask the same of them, depending upon our needs. Quite often I will get the student leadership together to give them factual, detailed information on matters that have been badly communicated or require further explanation. Frequently, I will ask for their positive influence on fellow peers in helping them make decisions or to better understand a program or policy.

GET PARENTS INVOLVED IN THE SCHOOLS

Generally, parents are involved with their children's schools until the high school years but then they fall out of touch. Of course, this happens because it's not "cool" for high school students to have their parents hanging around the school. Regardless of the grade level, autonomous school leaders who are team builders want parents in their schools. Parents in the school create a direct link to the people in the community, who generally rely on newspapers, radio, rumors, and innuendos for their information about the school. It is unlikely that we would find a strong administrative team that wasn't well supported by parents. By inviting parents to school to do volunteer work, substitute teaching, supervision of students, or classroom visitation, you are getting them invested directly. This is a lot more personal than a monthly newsletter and goes a long way in making friends and allies. In turn, parents who come to the school regularly will keep you informed as to what the current word is in the community. They will also do some important public relations work and, perhaps, help convert some of the more vocal naysayers.

CHAPTER 7

Climate Control: All Educators on Board

The culture of any school is determined by the attitude and behavior of the teaching staff. Students will follow their teachers' lead, behaving as they do both in and out of the classroom. Sarcastic, insubordinate teachers will breed the same kind of students, while those teachers who treat their students with dignity, respect, and consistency will forever bring out the best in them.

HOW, WHEN, AND WHY AMERICAN EDUCATION CHANGED

Once held in high esteem like physicians and other professionals, teachers enjoyed the support of the public who worked in harmony with them. Parents had confidence in their children's teachers and rarely questioned the methods used to educate or discipline. Students feared bringing home poor grades and reports of undesirable behavior, as the consequences would certainly be severe. Whatever the child did in school directly impacted the reputation of the family. Furthermore, parents were held accountable for the way their children behaved in school. Teachers performed their jobs much differently than they do today, in that they took direction from their administrators and school boards without question or resentment. Teachers' unions were nonexistent and issues related to insubordination and impropriety were minimal. For the most part, teachers worked in harmony with administrators. Veteran instructors especially were treated with respect and dignity by both their colleagues and superiors.

Generally speaking, teachers during these times entered the profession out of their passion for education and love of teaching. After all, it was a noble profession, where one could certainly make a difference in the lives of others. Contrary to what one may believe, wages and benefits for the average teacher were less reasonable than they are today. My mother, Concetta (Oliva) Brucato graduated from Boston University in 1941. She went on to Wellesley to complete her master's degree in Italian in 1942. Her first teaching contract for $1,200 per year was solidified only months after she left Wellesley. She was one of the few teachers available who had a master's degree, but this made no difference in her compensation, which amounted to about $24 a week. Sure, the dollar went a lot further in the 1940s, but a typical laborer with no education whatsoever could earn more than $24 a week.

My mother, who passed away at age 83, taught twenty-eight years before she retired in 1981 at age 61. Almost thirty years of service as a master language instructor; teaching Latin, French, Italian, and Spanish, Concetta left the profession earning $24,000 a year. Like most of her colleagues of that era, my mother witnessed firsthand the monumental changes in public education and the teaching profession. She did not, however, lose her focus, enthusiasm, or conscience for doing her job with excellence. Neither did she become cynical nor disheartened about the realities of an institution that was rapidly changing. Concetta was, in fact, a model educator and a team player. More importantly, she was a good colleague, forever sharing her talents as a gourmet cook with everyone she worked with at school. One example comes to mind in characterizing this devoted breed of educators. In 1978 as the demand for Spanish as a foreign language elective reduced the number of French teaching sections in her school, Concetta went back to college to learn Spanish, which she taught the last three years of her tenure.

When looking for an obvious beginning to the evolution of American public school education, most historians would agree that the 1960s, for many reasons, can be identified as the period that started things moving in a different direction. A changing economy, the Vietnam conflict, which turned family and friends against one another, along with a massive nationwide initiative to build new schools, would set in motion a reform movement that would continue to impact schools into the next century. A different breed of educators, the majority of whom were hired in the 1960s and 1970s would take on the personality of a society, which had lost its identity. American school cultures would from this point on be changed forever.

The teachers who entered the profession during these times did so for many different reasons. There were those who wanted an opportunity to continue their antiestablishment protests by educating American youth on the need to exercise their civil rights. Some became teachers because jobs were plentiful for college graduates, who were enticed by minimal requirements for certification. There were limited career opportunities available as the economy was struggling. This was especially true for women and minorities. Others entered the profession out of a sincere interest to make a difference, while some have admitted that they were not qualified or interested in doing anything else.

To make matters worse, the large number of teachers not coming from state teacher colleges were given little or no training on teaching methods, and had little, if any, experience working with young people. Unrest in schools, especially at the secondary level, became commonplace, as student protests caused teachers, sympathetic to the students, to take sides against their superiors. Parents in many households had lost their grip as peer influence and "flower power" pitted students against parental authority. The drug culture and sexual revolution added fuel to the fire, as did the many rock-and-roll icons, who gave American youth a needed comfort zone as well as a forum for self-expression. These issues, of course, were more dominant in our high schools, but lower-grade children felt the impact of the turmoil in their homes caused by rebellious older brothers and sisters. Teachers, as role models and authority figures, would continue to feel the impact of a generation of students committed to defying all aspects of the American establishment. Mistrust for civil and municipal employees was further exacerbated by Nixon's Watergate, which marked the beginnings of our nation's dirty laundry being aired publicly.

American educators, although battle weary, somehow managed to hold the line until it became evident that the American nuclear family, as we knew it, was a thing of the past. By the late 1970s, there were almost as many broken homes, with single parents, as there were two-parent homes. This, in my opinion at least, was the turning point for American educators and our entire system of education. Those subtle, nonviolent protests of the sixties and seventies gave way to the anger and violence of the eighties and nineties.

When I began teaching in 1978, I was fortunate to teach psychology as a social studies elective. With the curriculum tailored to adolescent issues, I had an opportunity to experience what students were feeling on a daily basis. Having the notoriety of being the youngest member of our teaching staff gave me an additional edge in gaining students' trust, as I had similar views on what was going on in our country. I remember my students as sixties "wannabes" with seemingly no original causes of their own. Oppositional, noncompliant, and apathetic behavior on the part of many students was commonplace, as was an increase in violent behavior by many angry teens. Many parents were at their wits' end, offering little help to the schools in deterring widespread misbehavior.

During a class discussion sometime in the early 1980s, I vividly remember a student putting the modern-day adolescent subculture into perspective, saying, "Our parents were part of the sixties thing and they pretty much sold out on us. After they cut their hair, sobered up, and put their protests behind them, the only lesson they had left for us was the importance of exercising one's civil rights and standing up for what you believe in. Then they let us be to figure it out on our own while they bought big homes and expensive cars. This is why we behave like we do."

The tide had most definitely turned. Students had changed, as did parents' views on education. Losing the battle on the home front, many parents conveniently transferred their blame to teachers and schools. Teachers, especially, became a convenient target for bashing. School boards under fire from disgruntled parents looked to school superintendents for answers, while superintendents, in turn, mandated to principals what they should do. In many cases, principals were forced to make decisions that left teachers feeling like their administrators made them even more vulnerable to public harangue.

Whenever this common scenario took hold during the 1980s and 1990s, the climate in school buildings worsened. Teachers' unions grew stronger and became more militant in negotiating contracts and working to the "rule" of those contracts. Ill feelings between administrators and teachers led to grievances and arbitrations. While underperforming or incompetent teachers used their unions and tenure to protect themselves, the morale among their dedicated hardworking colleagues sank to new lows. After all, the deadwood was taking home the same paycheck.

All this time, something even more critical was unfolding. The students, who had the most to lose, became the victims of this tragedy. Those students who were "fortunate" enough to have militant parents to fight the schools to get what they wanted, were enabled to remain underperforming and noncompliant. For those students who had no advocacy at home, it was even more tragic, as many would be deprived of educational opportunities while others would leave school without basic skills.

ENTER, "BREAKING RANKS, A NATION AT RISK"

Unfortunately, the smoke has yet to clear as state boards of education under pressure to keep our students in competition with their European and Asian counterparts have put a "full court press" on school districts nationwide. Teachers and administrators well on their way to retirement would be forced to rethink how students learn while using new, unfamiliar methods of instruction.

Ironically enough, teachers have had little to say about the reform movement, while students continue to remain the victims. In too many cases, demanding, hostile, and uncooperative parents continue to call the shots, sending their children the wrong messages. It is no wonder that our young people forever struggle with issues surrounding values and character. Research tells us that today's students generally think nothing of cheating and justify it as a means of survival in school.

Although building partnerships with parents is included in our reform package, it continues to be a one-way street. Teachers are still blamed for underperforming students and administrators are too often relegated to putting out fires and doing damage control. There are many days, as a principal, that I feel like donning a judge's robe for I am forever listening to evidence and appeals from the bench (my desk).

There are, of course, many other pieces to this complex puzzle. I chose a general overview of how social, political, and economic issues caused a difficult job to become more challenging and somewhat thankless to make a point. We can continue to blame history for degrading our profession and inhibiting our ability to teach children or we can wake up from the bad dream and accept responsibility for what we need to do for our children as educators of a new millennium.

Part III

NEW BEGINNINGS

Teachers need constant reminders as to why they chose to be teachers. The job of administrators is to keep teachers focused on their responsibilities, while minimizing distractions and holding them accountable for maintaining reasonable standards for their students. Additionally, school leaders must do whatever is necessary in preventing the teaching staff from becoming the enemy. Wounds of old, still open, must be closed, bad blood must be purged, and past practices that are no longer useful must be rethought.

Each and every issue that contributes to poor morale must be addressed. There are no issues too trivial to consider if they are important to the teachers. I've learned that it's the little things leaders do that go a long way toward improving the climate among the teaching staff. A short note of commendation for a job well done, or a simple "thank you" to acknowledge service to students and school can have a lasting effect on an uninspired instructor.

Remember that those teachers who became bitter, disillusioned, and unmotivated got that way because the leadership allowed it to happen.

It is just as easy to join forces with your teachers while getting them invested in school reform as it is to attempt to dictate to them via administrative directives. When teachers witness their leaders going to bat for them, they become willing to give more of themselves to the cause. Some teachers will require additional time and effort, as they have perhaps taken more of a beating over the years. In nearly every educator there is a still a good teacher, waiting to be reborn even after years of "losing one's soul."

Each faculty is different in terms of how long it will take to win their confidence and trust. This is why it is important to know the history of your school and those factors that contributed to the development of its culture. It will take much longer to make progress with a veteran faculty that spent most of its years in conflict with administration, as their mistrust is more deep-rooted. Regardless of the disposition of the teachers both individually and collectively, it will take time to mold them into a productive team, especially if they have not worked collaboratively with administration in the past.

A school leader will have countless opportunities to demonstrate to the faculty his sincerity in developing a culture where everyone has an opportunity to contribute to the success of the school. There are, however, some fundamental actions that leaders can perform to win the trust and support of the faculty.

GAINING FACULTY TRUST AND SUPPORT

"Actions Speak Louder than Words"

1. Keep your door open: never turn a teacher away.
2. Keep your word: tell the truth, don't make promises you can't keep.
3. Practice what you preach: be a good role model for teachers and they will be the same for students.
4. Compliment good deeds: don't let a day go by without thanking a teacher for a job well done.
5. Be visible in classrooms for reasons others than formal observations.
6. Act on requests in a timely manner: never leave teachers hanging; get back to them one way or another.
7. Mend fences: after disagreements take some time to regroup, revisit, and reestablish relationships.
8. Keep faculty informed of their colleague's good fortunes and misfortunes.
9. Take a personal interest in each and every member of the faculty: make it a point to know what's going on in their lives. Send cards, notes, make inquiries.
10. Look for opportunities to praise "groups" of faculty members to reinforce the importance of collaborative efforts.

CHAPTER 8

Swinging the Balance

Most educational leaders would agree that a teaching staff, regardless of its size, will have some outstanding teachers, some who are underperforming, and others who can go either way depending upon how they are influenced. For the purpose of assessing the strengths and weaknesses of a faculty, it's convenient to break things down into approximate thirds. The top third would include those teachers who are regarded as excellent instructors, considered as such by students, parents, and members of the community. The middle third is represented by those teachers who have shown signs of excellence but have been inconsistent and somewhat reluctant to put the time in necessary for top echelon notoriety. The bottom third consists of those teachers who have lost their purpose, were never effective to begin with, do not command respect from students and colleagues, or just can't seem to bring out anything but the worst in their students.

The strength of the leadership will determine if, in fact, the middle tier of instructors are pushed into the top echelon or allowed to be dragged down by their underperforming colleagues. Swinging the balance is by no means an easy task, as negative individuals on the faculty are forever looking for vulnerable prey, while the model instructors tend to do their jobs while keeping to themselves. The leadership, therefore, must know the players, identify the most influential member of the faculty, and take deliberate measures in isolating the malcontents while challenging the top performers on the staff to become active, vocal leaders among their colleagues.

It has been my experience that the good ones will be more than happy to work with the leadership in reposturing the faculty, as long as the leadership can demonstrate that they mean business. Winning the respect and support of your top echelon teachers is simply a matter of making their nonconformist colleagues do their jobs according to specifications. The "climate killers," as I call them, do a major injustice to their responsible colleagues each and every time they decide to ignore the rules. By insisting that every member of the faculty is accountable and promptly taking a progressive course of disciplinary action with those teachers who are the noncompliant, you are vindicating the "good soldiers" who will more than likely make more of an effort to help the cause.

Many administrators, historically, have consciously chosen not to deal with malcontents simply because they do not want the aggravation, or lack the confidence in their ability to effectively isolate these people. Educational leaders committed to improving the climate in their buildings are obligated to deal with the "naysayers," as they are dangerous and destructive members of the faculty. Isolating these individuals is a matter of personally letting them know where they stand and what might become of their teaching/supervisory assignments if they continue to violate the team. I prefer the "fireside chat" method of communicating expectations, but you might prefer the hand-delivered, "frank-and-open memo" to make clear your expectations and concerns. Whatever the method, be sure to spell out the consequences and be ready to follow through if the undesirable behavior persists. Keep in mind that even though faculty malcontents have a right to voice their opinion, the administrator is empowered to judge behavior as "unprofessional" or "insubordinate." For those crafty teachers who seem, deliberately, to just barely keep from crossing the line, you reserve the right to act on each and every breach of contractual responsibility no matter how trivial. In dealing with these unhappy individuals, who are no doubt making students unhappy, you are sending a powerful message to the entire school community. "If you don't want to play on the team, consider your options! If you don't like your options, figure out how you're going to change the picture."

What the leadership does to motivate the middle-echelon teachers to become more consistent and accountable is even more critical, as the ultimate goal is to drive the masses upward. When this happens, the remaining underperforming teachers are exposed, increasing the probability that they will either improve or begin looking for a new situation.

An abundance of praise, encouragement, and specific plans for improvement are most effective in helping your middle-tier teachers perform to their potential. Offering a variety of professional development opportunities, teaming them with excellent colleagues, or having them observe teachers both in-house and in other schools are all effective initiatives. By investing in these teachers, while taking a personal interest in their professional growth, you gain their confidence and trust.

When the climate improves among the faculty, you have effectively swung the balance. If the process seems to be moving along too slowly, do not give in to the frustration. Stay the course and remember that this is just one more battle you fight in the best interests of your students. When teachers are motivated and content, students reap the benefits of enhanced instruction in a stable, comfortable environment.

CHAPTER 9

Clarity of Expectations

When administrative leadership teams meet during the summer months, they have an opportunity to assess faculty performance as it relates to the expectations established for the prior school year.

A thorough analysis of problematic situations resulting from negligence on the part of faculty members or an unwillingness on their part to carry out certain responsibilities, can help leadership teams determine if in fact, expectations were clear as well as reasonable. Perhaps the expectations were too ambitious, ambiguous, or miscommunicated. Whatever the findings, they will serve as the basis for developing expectations for the upcoming school year.

Teachers need to be reminded of the many "routine" responsibilities, that if neglected by even a small faction of individuals, cause problems for everyone. Expectations are somewhat different than Key Responsibility Areas in that teachers will be challenged, on a daily basis, to either address all of these things or conveniently choose to ignore the ones they don't want to be bothered with. Expectations are developed to raise levels of consciousness and have value in promoting unity among teachers. The ultimate goal of well-defined expectations, which can change from year to year, is to make each and every member of the faculty accountable to one another. If you have a very large building, like ours, where the faculty is organized by departments, teachers naturally become isolated from many of their colleagues, while staying close to their home base (the department office and their classroom).

By establishing clear and concise expectations, which require teachers to work collaboratively, service students with consistency, while assuming responsibility for everything that goes on in the building, the leadership is actively engaged in developing the culture of the faculty, which in turn permeates throughout the student body.

MILFORD HIGH SCHOOL: FACULTY EXPECTATIONS

1. All faculty members will be 99 percent accurate in keeping records, both in homeroom and individual classes (human error would allow for one mistake).
2. All faculty members will consistently follow procedures established in the Milford High School Faculty Manual and Student/ Parent Handbook.
3. All faculty and staff will look for opportunities to integrate the mission of Milford High School into their teaching lessons and interactions with students.
4. All faculty and staff members will contribute to the initiative to improve school climate through character education and higher expectations for student decorum, dress, communications, etc.
5. All faculty members will complete a minimum of ten hours of professional development in authentic assessment practices.
6. All faculty members will read and understand the School Improvement Plan and contribute to those initiatives that are identified as "teacher" responsibilities.
7. All faculty members will teach their course curriculum as it is written. A pacing guide and curriculum map where applicable should be used and will be incorporated into the observation/ evaluation process.
8. All faculty and staff members will work collaboratively in the supervision of our building for the purpose of preventing problems and reporting information.
9. All faculty and staff members will contribute to the aesthetic enhancement of our building by keeping their personal classrooms and work areas clean, orderly, and free of clutter. Vandalism and maintenance needs will be reported in a timely manner.
10. All faculty members will assume assigned supervision duties between their contracted morning starting time and the first teaching

block. Homeroom teachers will remain outside of their home-rooms (in the corridor) until the first bell sounds and all students are out of the corridor.

11. All faculty members will make an effort to help one another solve problems.

CHAPTER 10

The Faculty Manual

Each and every school district has a policy manual, which usually sits on a remote shelf collecting dust in various administrative offices. The policies, many of which were written decades ago, providing general guidelines for all divisions within the district, are rarely visited unless a unique situation forces a school leader to go to the book. Changes in state laws over the years have crammed one addendum after another into the already-cumbersome binder, while few teachers, if any, have ever had knowledge of its existence. If the manual was useful and revised annually, then I dare say, it wouldn't take two people to lift it off its shelf!

A faculty manual, on the other hand, is essential for all schools in that it gives teachers a specific protocol to follow for every possible situation that may come about. School policies and procedures, along with faculty responsibilities can be coherently organized in this manual, giving teachers a valuable and useful tool. Unlike the district manual, the faculty manual must be constantly updated, revised, and edited. For new teachers, the faculty manual is critical, and for all teachers, it serves as the basis for establishing the agenda for the full faculty meeting that kicks off a new school year.

At the conclusion of each school year, one of my assistants is assigned the task of revising the faculty manual. The task is not all that arduous, as throughout the school year we keep notes on those policies or procedures that require revision. Each member of the faculty turns in his or her manual at the conclusion of the school year. The newly revised manual is returned to teachers in September, when we meet for orientation.

The manual provides another useful opportunity to assess the needs of the faculty while ensuring that teachers have a clear understanding of the numerous policies they are required to follow. Unlike the Student/Parent Handbook, which outlines behavior standards for the students, the Faculty Manual addresses such issues as preparing for substitutes, evacuating the building, dealing with oppositional students, and reporting harassment.

Key Responsibility Areas (KRAs) for faculty will serve as the foundation for the manual. The KRAs are very specific, giving administrators and teachers a ready-made performance evaluation tool. These can be found at the end of this chapter. When teachers fail to perform any of their KRAs or are inconsistent in any given area, corrective action should be taken immediately.

KEY RESPONSIBILITY AREAS FOR FACULTY

Punctuality—Be on time all the time and expect the same from students.

Attendance—Begin each class period by taking accurate attendance. Turn in your A.M. attendance roster at the conclusion of homeroom period. Check the daily attendance bulletin for tardiness and dismissals. Send cut slips at the end of each day. Scrutinize the attendance bulletin, and then send cut slips.

Teach-Assigned Curriculum—Follow the objectives of the current curriculum guide for the specific course. Continue to revise and make current all curriculums, working cooperatively with other members of your department. Have a working knowledge of the curriculum frameworks and how the strands apply to your lessons.

Carry Out Supervisory Duties If and When Assigned—We hurt one another and give mixed messages to our students when one does and one doesn't perform his/her duties.

Enforce General School Policies—There are no exceptions to the rules. *Hats* in the building when on people's heads are not acceptable. All *foods* are to be eaten in the cafeteria, and all canned and bottled *drinks* should be consumed there. *Coffee* and other Bistro products can be enjoyed by faculty members in the Bistro, cafeteria, or in the privacy of one's departmental office. *Smoking* is not allowed in the building or on school grounds—period!

Enforce School Grading Policy—As long as the guidelines call for four major tests or evaluations on grades per marking period, then four should be given. Students should be made aware of the grading policy from day one. When the grading policy is made clear and enforced consistently, problems are minimized.

Communicate with Parents—This, in most cases, is the best way to get results when student performance or conduct is subpar or unacceptable. A progress report is a formality for the teacher's protection. A call to a parent is an expression of concern and compassion for the student. Communicate with parents in the same manner you expect teachers of your own children to communicate with you. Please call parent/guardian *immediately* when student performance or conduct is subpar or unacceptable.

Classroom Decorum—Acceptable classroom decorum evolves from the teacher's leading by example and making clear which behaviors are acceptable and which ones are not. Different teachers run their classrooms differently, but there are some basic things that are not acceptable in any classroom. Off-color language, harassment, and lack of conformity by a student that disrupts the learning process or creates anxiety for other students is not to be tolerated. Consistency and early intervention again are the keys here. If you have discipline problems, remember that they are much more effectively dealt with by you. Utilize parents/guardians as a resource.

Develop Standards and Policies for Your Classroom and Students—Make clear all standards and expectations. Distribute a letter addressed to parents/guardian on the first day of school that details classroom procedures and standards.

Communicate with Colleagues, Administrators, and Students—Make no assumptions and give no expectations! If you want something, ask for it. If you have a complaint involving another colleague, take it up with him or her in private. If we want people to be up front and honest with us, we must behave in a way to make that happen.

Protect the Confidentiality of Your Students—Students' grades, personal problems, or special circumstances are between you and the student. Students should never grade one another's papers or see one another's grades. Keep rank books in your personal possession or in a secure place at all times.

Read and Process All Individual Education Plans and 504 Plans— Know the provisions of each individual plan and make necessary accommodations. Respond to all requests from the guidance and special education departments in an appropriate and timely manner. Attend review meetings if possible.

Read Memorandums—Pay attention to detail. Be aware of due dates so that you may get things done in a timely manner. Keep your students informed of any pertinent information and changes in the daily routine.

Keep Students in the Classroom—Corridor and bathroom passes should be used with discretion and students should never be put out of class for minor behavioral occurrences. Do not send students to the office for discipline during class time. If you feel the situation is out of control, call an administrator to come to your classroom.

Reporting—The following should be reported with consistency and regularity. These are the critical procedural things that make our jobs easy when they are done by all.

Daily

- Students absent from class—check all lists, absence, tardy, dismissed before sending slips.
- Students present in class but *on* the absent list.
- Students smoking on school grounds.
- Students leaving school grounds during school hours.
- Cheating.
- Vandalism.
- Fighting

Other

Harassment—If you witness a student being harassed by another or are made aware that a student is being harassed, it should be reported immediately to an administrator, guidance counselor, or adjustment counselor.

Fighting—Do everything in your power to stop the fighting without jeopardizing your own health, but be sure to report all incidents to house principals immediately; always follow up with a written report.

Abuse—If you are made aware of a student being abused either directly or indirectly, you are obligated, by law, to report it. Report all suspected abuse to school nurse or adjustment counselors.

Accidents—Any and all accidents should be reported to the school nurse who will prepare a report for the principal and fill out the proper insurance forms.

Excessive Tardies—Address students who are chronically tardy in a consistent manner. Follow discipline procedures for excessive tardies.

Supervision of Students—NEVER LEAVE STUDENTS UNSUPERVISED. If you have an emergency, make sure a colleague is available to supervise your class. If not, call for an administrator.

Excessive Absence of Students—Five consecutive days or any irregular pattern should be reported to house principals and guidance counselors.

Distraught or Anxious Students—If you are at all suspicious or in the least bit concerned that a student may want to hurt himself or herself, play it safe and report it immediately to the adjustment counselor, school nurse, or an administrator.

Theft—Report whatever you know to an administrator immediately.

My administrative team uses what I would consider a very fair approach in helping remind teachers that KRAs are not negotiable. A first offense elicits a verbal reminder, whereas a second infraction is addressed in a Memorandum of Concern. If a teacher persists in being negligent with any given KRA a third time, that teacher will be asked to attend a meeting with administrators. The meeting will serve to develop an improvement plan that will be included in the formal evaluation of that teacher. For underperforming instructors, improvement plans are absolutely imperative, as they remove subjectivity from the evaluation process while giving teachers very specific strategies and objectives to follow.

By placing the onus on the teacher to improve in deficient areas, while working with that instructor in the development of a plan, you are giving needed credibility to the evaluation process. Just as teachers unions have language and instruments to protect their members, administrators in all schools are empowered to follow a process, which will lead to the improvement or termination of underperforming teachers.

Many school leaders would rather position a poor teacher in their schools where they can do the least amount of damage, rather than spend the time necessary to help improve or move them out. Teachers unions were not created to protect incompetent teachers. When this happens, and we all know it does, valued members of the teachers union are just as frustrated and resentful as parents, administrators, and school boards.

For an administrator inheriting a host of poor teachers, it's a convenient excuse to resolve that nothing can be done with them because of prior years of favorable evaluations. This, of course, is a "cop-out" and as much of a misconception as tenure or professional status making incompetent teachers untouchable. Just as negligent, lazy students can be motivated to perform by good teachers, lazy, negligent teachers can be made to improve by an effective school leader. Like students, teachers do not like to be caught acting out of character, being reprimanded for negligent acts, or disciplined for breaking the rules.

Administrators unwilling to take on incompetent teachers are failing their students, parents, and hardworking members of the faculty. To be an educational leader, you must always place the students first. In not working to make underperforming employees better, you are cheating your students and overworking your best teachers who invariably have to pick up the slack.

School leaders need to know the specifics of the teachers union contract better than the teachers, especially those sections of the contract dealing with teaching responsibilities. By extracting specific paragraphs from the contract and placing them in the faculty manual, you are reminding teachers of specific key responsibility areas that they, as union members, have agreed to fulfill. We used the following, for example:

TEACHING DUTIES

The School Committee and Association acknowledges that a teacher's primary responsibility is to educate children and to help them learn, and the main focus of his/her energies and professional assignment should be those school-day activities that deal directly with education and learning. The Committee and Association mutually recognize, therefore, that teachers should be primarily utilized in the following areas:

1. The preparation, presentation, and evaluation of lessons;
2. The management of their classroom and the care of equipment and material contained therein;
3. The supervision of students placed in their charge;
4. The maintenance of records directly related to classroom instruction;
5. The counseling and guidance of students, especially those within their classes:
6. The performance of all other duties relevant to the development of systems and programs relegated to a teacher's area of instruction.

By doing this, school leaders are using the contract to their advantage. Underperforming teachers can regularly be cited for negligence of any of the specific duties outlined in their contract. When poor teachers realize that the very language of their contract can be used against them, they will more than likely change or look for another school system that doesn't demand accountability. Of course, they can choose to be resistant to change, in which case the school leader can "evaluate them out" of the system.

School administrators who are persistent but patient can rid their schools of poor teachers. They must, however, be willing to spend the time it takes, while following a well-designed, methodical process.

When developing a faculty manual, no stone should be left unturned. Additionally, the manual should be written like curriculum guides that are living, breathing, documents and are effective only if they are revisited frequently and revised regularly.

CHAPTER 11

Growth and Excellence Are Not Optional

Educational leaders who want their schools to be excellent will work within the procedures and frameworks of their districts to make it happen. Climate-focused leaders are especially preoccupied with the objective of achieving excellence as they know that until they get beyond the mediocrity their teachers have come to accept, it will be business as usual.

Veteran teachers especially are uncomfortable with change and many of them are not willing to do their part in making reform initiatives work. It is too convenient for them to remain in a "comfort zone" while thinking of every possible reason why change is not necessary or that specific reforms won't work. They also like to play the role of the victim, blaming everyone from state legislators to school boards to parents for making it impossible for them to effectively do their jobs. Teachers love to make the claim that nobody ever asks them what's good for schools or students and therefore rationalize that it is their responsibility to resist change.

There is, however, a hidden agenda, which becomes evident in dialogue with educators who in their infinite criticism of educational reform, reveal that change is not good for them. Just listen to teachers talk about their job and you can understand this. They will talk about their courses, their classroom, their materials, their methods, their schedule, and their expectations. What's wrong with this picture? The needs of the students are somehow not factored into the equation. The last time I checked, it was the responsibility of the teacher to meet the needs of the students. One thing is for certain; until the "I" is extinguished from the teacher vocabulary, change initiatives will remain futile. This "egocentric attitude" is obviously most prevalent among veteran educators who are frightened of change and are concerned about how it might threaten their comfort zone or increase their workload. It will take more than an attitude adjustment hour to get your teachers out of this mindset, but like everything else in this business, a purposeful plan of attack will bring results.

When I became a principal, I began my tenure by making it clear to my teachers that they would be reminded frequently that we will do what we need to do in the best interest of our students. I also informed them that they do not have deeds to classrooms or rights to specific courses or assignments. It was imperative that all teachers understood student needs as primary in determining teaching assignments. Along the same lines, I would ask my teachers to assume an active role in the annual review of course offerings in the various curricular areas. If new courses have to replace "teacher-favorite electives" in the best interest of students, then they should be prepared to teach those courses.

The next thing my faculty would hear is that we would remain focused on the mission of achieving excellence in all curricular and co-curricular areas, while paying little or no attention to those things beyond our control. Realizing that it would be my responsibility to keep my faculty focused, I was prepared to run interference for them by doing whatever is necessary to prove that we were in fact running our school. We would establish our own goals and get what we needed to fulfill our responsibilities to the students by following a process. I am no different than the next school leader in advocating for my school, but more importantly, I have learned that you can get whatever you need if you are willing to do the work necessary to validate your needs. Achieving excellence requires a focus and an attitude that all members of the faculty must adopt. By recognizing regularly all of the good things that students do that are a result of good teaching, the leadership keeps the faculty focused on the positives. I look for every possible opportunity to praise students, teachers, and staff for their accomplishments while inspiring them to continually strive for excellence.

EXCELLENCE

Striving for excellence becomes an attitude, which is driven by conscience. We are challenged every day to be prepared and on top of our game. There are many critics and few who come forward to sing our praises for the many good deeds we do for our students. We must remain focused on our goal to educate with excellence and never stop striving for the best effort our students can give us, both in the classroom and in the school community.

When our students are recognized for their excellence in both academic and cocurricular areas, it is because they had excellent teachers and role models to pave the way.

Many of our excellent performances in the classroom, gestures of kindness toward students, and hours of supervision in and out of the classroom are not acknowledged and appreciated by our many critics, but I do believe that the students and administration know just what teachers do to make us excellent.

The striving for excellence is demonstrated in the many things teachers do on a daily basis in the name of their schools.

The striving for excellence is a beginning, but achieving excellence is the means to the end. Nothing of value can be achieved without hard work and dedication. Therefore, my teachers would need to learn that personal and professional growth is not an option. By enunciating this law, I was prepared to be a role model, while providing the faculty with purposeful, pertinent, professional development opportunities. When we began the monstrous task of rewriting curriculum in all disciplines to bring it in line with the state frameworks, it was important that curriculum mapping was inclusive in the initiative. Pacing guides for each individual course would also be essential in maintaining the integrity of the curriculum and prompting regular revisions. Many of my teachers were not familiar with mapping and pacing curriculum, so I would become a student of Heidi Jacobs and lead the way. A local college was happy to sponsor a graduate course that I developed for my teachers, titled, "Standards-Based Teaching and Curriculum Mapping." The course was well attended as it was held in our school within a schedule that my teachers chose.

There would be no more "dog and pony" shows or days off for teachers to chase Professional Development Points at the "one-shot-deal" workshop with no follow-up. Recertification needs would not determine our course of action either, at least not on school time. I am not a fan of contrived personal improvement plans, as they too offer no benefits to the students. My philosophy regarding professional development is quite simple: "Show me how your students and colleagues will benefit from the initiative, and I will finance it." Veteran educators are especially resistant to professional development activities, since many feel, having only a few years left, they should be exempt.

If the goal of professional development is to make teachers better instructors for the benefit of students, school leaders are obligated to monitor the process. Historically, many teachers have engaged in professional development activities to make salary schedule hurdles, taking the lines of least resistance and wasting valuable school dollars. Every school has "workshop kings and queens," who if not watched closely, will take more professional days than a consultant. (The students, of course, will pay the price for the absentee teacher, but they will have the benefit of bonding with every substitute teacher in the district!) Changing this picture will require not only the work of the school leadership but the collective efforts of the district administrative team.

In our school system, all of our principals, under the direction of our assistant superintendent, are responsible for developing a K–12 professional development plan with a conscience. In drafting the plan, we agree to focus all of our professional development offerings for the upcoming school year on three or four needs, that are essential for all of our teachers, regardless of the grade level. Our assistant superintendent, a former principal, serves as our team leader and curriculum council coordinator. He keeps us focused on the task of proving out our needs, while insisting that, once we agree on the plan, no school leader is to stray off course. Additionally, he insists that all upcoming in-service and contractual days will involve activities for teachers based on chosen needs, until such time that we decide as a team that our needs have changed. To ensure the integrity of the process and accountability for our teachers regarding the chosen professional development initiatives, all principals will include specific references documenting the level of participation or a lack thereof in each individual teacher evaluation.

Finally, all principals, as members of the district leadership team, will participate in a mutually agreed-upon graduate course designed to meet our collective needs while giving us a regularly scheduled opportunity to collaborate and grow stronger as a team.

This purposeful approach to professional development can be successfully employed in any school district that believes, as we do, that teachers need to understand what's going on in the grade levels below and above them in order to properly fulfill the needs of their students. Additionally, when teachers within the system perceive their district leadership team as a unified body committed to professional growth, they are more likely to come on board than they are to suffer the consequences of nonconformity.

CHAPTER 12

Teacher Appreciation

The final step in bringing teachers on board to improve school climate will require the leadership to demonstrate sincere appreciation for teachers throughout the school year. Social gatherings, which give the faculty an opportunity to bond informally, will also do wonders in renewing collegial relationships and creating new ones.

The annual Teacher Appreciation Day sponsored by the student leadership is a wonderful activity. It does not, however, serve to convince teachers that they are well thought of and appreciated by many, simply because they are teachers. For some strange reason, students, parents, and administrators often forget to thank their teachers for hard work, dedication, and kind deeds. On the other hand, a day rarely goes by when teachers don't hear something negative said about them or about their profession. Low self-esteem and defensive behavior are commonly acquired characteristics of any human being who is constantly put down or degraded. Why should it be any different for American public school teachers who are forever bashed by anyone and everyone capable of throwing verbal stones? (Of course, these stones are being thrown from glass houses, but that's another story altogether.)

Climate-focused school leaders look for every possible opportunity to either show appreciation or inspire others to acknowledge the good deeds of their teachers. Gestures of appreciation need not be extravagant or costly, but they must always be heartfelt and sincere. This is one area, also, that the leadership never has to worry about overkill. In fact, the more you keep teachers focused on the good things they are doing, the less time they have to dwell on negatives.

This basic behaviorist approach in no way discounts the importance of nurturing the human soul, even though it employs the methods of what behaviorists refer to as "conditioning." By giving teachers more opportunities to feel good about themselves in the work place, you are helping to metamorphose their avoidance behaviors into a tendency to do more things well because they are positively reinforced.

While many of your appreciation initiatives will be planned, those that occur spontaneously are equally effective.

Two years ago when it was obvious that my faculty was tired and not looking forward to an upcoming in-service day workshop, I decided to change gears. As they filed into the auditorium that day prepared for one of those long "sleep-with-your-eyes-open" workshops, they were in store for a surprise. Instead of the planned activity, they would be treated to a one-hour concert by a popular *a cappella* group who sang hit songs from the '50s and '60s. When the hour was over, I thanked my faculty for the good work they were doing and dismissed them early. Needless to say, they were thankful, appreciative, and came to school the next day happy and somewhat renewed. Who picked up the tab you ask? The student leadership council was more than happy to foot the bill and take credit for the sponsorship of this appreciation event.

Serving *coffee and refreshments at faculty meetings* on occasion is inexpensive and always well received, especially at the end of a school day when teachers are spent. They are thankful and show their gratitude by being well behaved and attentive. "Feed your faculty and make them your friends!"

At the conclusion of each school year, I will gather the faculty together for closure. An appreciation plaque is presented to all teachers retiring, including a recapping of their careers. Of course, we capitalize on the opportunity to "roast" those more flamboyant, outgoing veterans. A light lunch of pizza or sandwiches is served along with the ceremonial year's end cake. Concluding the year on a high note is important for everyone, but especially significant for those who will not be returning for another year.

Teachers also appreciate the efforts of the leadership in promoting collegiality and respect among colleagues. We regularly inform the faculty of news concerning all employees in the building. It's much easier, of course, to celebrate the joyous occasions like births, weddings, and retirements, but those sad occasions involving loss of family or friends must also be included so that colleagues can offer condolences. Whatever the occasion or event, faculty and staff will receive an informative memo explaining the circumstances.

The most significant appreciation initiative, however, is the letter of commendation or note of thanks. My leadership team understands the value of reinforcing those behaviors that are not only exceptional, but noteworthy because someone expressed gratitude for a teacher's deeds. When we hear about or witness good deeds, we acknowledge them with either personal notes of thanks or formal commendations, depending on the circumstances. There are no good deeds too small to acknowledge.

An often-overlooked appreciation gesture is the leadership's effort to create equity among the faculty by regularly acknowledging the value of all departments and course offerings. If the core areas are forever getting all of the attention, while practical arts, fine arts, physical education, business, and music continue to take the hits, the leadership is allowing those noncore area teachers to become second-class citizens in the school.

By working to keep each and every program strong, the leadership is sending a message. I have made it clear to my faculty that there will be no sacrificial lambs. All of our programs would be kept strong and have the advocacy of the administration. When the MCAS (Massachusetts Competency Assessments) became a reality, many schools in Massachusetts have made mathematics and language arts a priority. Enrichment and remediation programs in mathematics and English have caused many districts throughout the state to scale down other programs in order to finance these initiatives.

To make a faculty "one," each individual and program has to have value in the eyes of the leadership. More importantly, the leadership must publicly acknowledge the accomplishments of all programs. Everything we do at our school that is noteworthy is placed in the local newspaper. In many cases we write our own press releases and take our own pictures. The weekly faculty bulletin and daily use of the public address system enables us to constantly publicize events, congratulate people for achievements, and thank faculty and staff for their efforts.

BONDING

Faculty and staff bonding activities are easy to organize and provide opportunities for colleagues to enjoy one another's company in a setting other than the school building. This is especially important for large schools where some colleagues might never cross paths during the school year.

We have had a faculty golf tournament for many years now. This "not for golfers only" best ball tournament mixes accomplished golfers with those who have never held a golf club. Teams of four or five play nine holes of golf and then retire to a local establishment for a family-style meal. A celebrity roast follows the meal, while team and door prizes are handed out to round out the evening. You can run your tournament in the fall or spring with the same results. "The faculty that plays together, stays together." Administrators, faculty, staff, and even former members of the school community are invited to carry on a tradition that everyone involved looks forward to.

If your school has bowling enthusiasts, you can host a tournament in the same manner at the local alleys, be they ten or candle pins. The more gutter balls, the more laughs! Besides, most participants are more interested in the food, drink, and camaraderie that follows.

Faculty *versus* students athletic contests are another way to bring people together in your school. Our student leadership council sponsors a spirit week to kick off each new school year. The week concludes with an "all-sports" rally in the gymnasium where the entire student body, faculty, and staff assemble for a brief spirit program introducing the captains of all sports. The band and cheerleaders raise the noise level while sections of freshmen, sophomores, juniors, and seniors compete for the most spirited class. Students selected by lottery then play a "no holds barred" game of basketball against a team of faculty and administrators. Student commentators do the play-by-play, taking good-natured digs at teachers who willingly go out on the floor to show their total lack of athletic skills.

Hiring a bus for a trip to the nearest casino, the theater, or for a "mystery ride" is another popular activity for bringing people together. The bus trip to wherever is a perfect time for drinks, finger foods, and all the laughs you can manage. It also makes for a great opportunity to have a trivia contest. Hand out "gag" awards or just let everyone aboard enjoy one another's company. Yellow buses are out of the question! Pay the extra money for the luxury coach and enjoy the evening in style.

Faculty and staff luncheons sponsored by the leadership council, to either kick off or conclude a school year, will be well attended and critical in setting the tone for a new year or bringing closure to a year gone by. These are the forums appropriate for the welcome of new employees and/or paying tribute to those retiring. Agendas for these events should be brief, as you want to give all of your employees time to eat, drink, and mingle.

Forming a social committee made up of faculty and staff members is a great way to get started in planning a social calendar for faculty and staff.

There are any number of activities to consider when deciding what will bring the biggest draw for your group. One thing is certain, if you want good attendance, charge no admission!

CHAPTER 13

The Student Body: The Driving Force of School Reform

"It will do us no good to complain about the dysfunctional, high-maintenance students in our school because these are our players . . . the community's not sending us the second team."

—Donald Gainey

As educators nationally are scrambling to meet the needs of school reform mandates conjured up by politicians, state boards of education, and pseudo-educators, it's easy to understand why even the most intuitive school leaders lose touch with the student body. The students, in many districts, are the guinea pigs or play things, who are victimized by in-vogue initiatives marketed by the "one-size-fits-all" research studies we are expected to accept as gospel. How many times have you heard of a school leader holding true to his convictions by refusing to do what is mandated because it's not in the best interest of his students? Chances are, if you know one of these folk heroes, they are probably still out looking for another job.

School administrators complain of facing a job with unreasonable demands and an overwhelming amount of stress. As a public high school principal, I might have every reason to feel this way; however, I have chosen not to because, as I explained earlier, I choose not to be a victim. More significant than that is a philosophy I have adopted that has simplified my occupational existence. What it boils down to is this:

Whatever I do, I do in the best interest of the student body as a whole. I do not cater to special interests, succumb to political pressure, concern myself with who won't be happy, or worry about becoming unpopular with teachers or parents. Therefore, I make the tough decisions less difficult by keeping my focus on the needs of the students.

Effectively ministering to the student body will require the same in-depth assessment of the culture and climate of the school in the areas of student behavior and perceptions. There are a number of factors that influence the behavior, attitudes, and perceptions of the student body. There are, however, some very important variables that require considerable attention from school leaders when they become committed to building a safe, healthy, positive school climate that is student centered. These variables, I believe, can become the guiding principles that keep school leaders forever focused on maintaining a well-run school where the needs of all students are met. If one is, as I am, committed to meeting these objectives, then one must be dedicated to the cause of placing the students first and demonstrating through deeds, not words, that you are sincere in your desire to ensure that these variables are given the attention they require.

THE LINE IN THE SAND

There are a number of university-based research studies that claim that the more strict the discipline in a given school, the poorer the climate in the student body. We all know, however, that those who do "outside-in" research have little to no experience in dealing with everyday, complex student discipline issues.

I agree with the fact that most punishments are not very effective; therefore, I choose to spend time and energy educating my students on the consequences of their actions. This is done by making clear the expectations for student behavior and then "drawing a line in the sand." Some schools choose to create what they call "zero-tolerance" policies, which in essence become "low tolerance" as soon as the first student finds a loophole in the policy, making it impossible for consequences to be administered. Each time this happens, schools and administrations lose credibility with their students, who will then take their chances when choosing to behave contrary to expectations. (Such policies are also notably poor at addressing the unusual offense or unexpected set of circumstances—the first grader with the licorice gun, etc.)

Contrary to what some may think, students, especially teenagers, want to know what they can and can't do. More importantly, they demand that the same consequences be applicable to all members of the student body, regardless of who they are or what roles they assume in the school.

Students at all levels will usually test the system, capitalizing on every contradiction or precedent they can identify to break the rules and circumvent the consequences. What has made matters worse, for teachers and school leaders especially, is the number of parents who enable their children to become noncompliant, by helping them fight the school instead of working with school officials to address the reasons for the undesirable behavior.

By placing the responsibility on students to behave in a way that is consistent with the mission of the school, school leaders refuse to be made victims of unacceptable student behavior. The effectiveness of this approach lies in the ability of school leaders to demonstrate, through their actions, that this is the way it's going to be. When the line is crossed, the student will, like it or not, accept the consequences for his or her actions as long as these consequences were made clear to them at the outset of the year. Student offenders and blindly supportive parents love to point fingers and place blame when it comes to having to do the time for the crime. How many times have you heard the cry, "They suspended me" or "He ruined my life" or "She caused me to get thrown off the team"? On the other hand, how many times have you had the experience of witnessing a decision to administer consequences reversed because of pressure exerted on teachers and school leaders? These concessions become the kiss of death, and the very reason why the same ugly situations will continue to be repeated, over and over again. As I like to remind teachers, "The value of trust can only be learned when young people realize that there are consequences for violating that trust."

By drawing a line in the sand, making consequences clear, and holding your ground, I guarantee that the frequency of, and time spent on, student discipline issues will be dramatically decreased.

The best example I can offer you involves a senior class tradition that existed at our school for many years, placing students in danger, disrupting the school community, and causing administrators grief and hours of wasted time.

The night before the seniors' last day of school, an all-night "beer bash" would be held at an undisclosed location. Most members of the class would attend and participate in the "vigil" as it had become a tradition. The students would decorate their cars, paint their faces, and after a long night of drinking, would form a caravan of cars. The large parade of cars with intoxicated students blaring their horns, hanging out of windows, or standing up in crowded convertibles or truck bodies would begin in the hours preceding school opening. The multi-car caravan would eventually weave its way in and out of school grounds while teachers and other school officials held their breath. There was always an accident of some sort, but fortunately, none I remember as life threatening. Once the students were corralled into the building, a day of pure hell, which seemed never ending, would result in damage to the building, multiple suspensions, and harassment of underclassmen. The seniors called this day "Freshman Friday," as ninth graders, especially, would be the target of bullying seniors who felt entitled to literally terrorize underclassmen. To make matters worse, most of these seniors were intoxicated and their judgment was poor at best. Fortunately, no one was ever killed or seriously hurt.

When I became the principal of the school, I made it clear that this tradition would come to an end. With the help of my assistants and teachers who were totally behind me, we drew the line in the sand. Letters were sent home to parents and meetings held with the seniors. The superintendent and school board were supportive and prepared to respond to any student, parent, or other member of the community who acted in defiance of our expectations.

Regardless of our interventions, it was clear that the tradition would continue, but it would also end with the class of 1999. As the day drew closer and students continued to plan their gala event right under our noses, we were fortunate enough to influence a number of our student leaders to make the right choice. The police department had pledged their support and the chief added patrol details. We met with the seniors one last time and I explained to them that any senior deciding to carry out old traditions would lose all senior privileges including prom, awards, and senior night.

I received a call at 2:00 A.M. from the police department, indicating that some thirty-five of my seniors were being booked and would be arraigned in the district court at 8:00 A.M. Most were charged as minors in possession of alcohol and disorderly conduct. By the way, these were the thirty-five who didn't run when the police arrived. There was a whole lot more to the story and the many complex scenarios surrounding the incident. What is most important for you to know, however, is that by investing my time and energy in preventive discipline, it made what I had to do become easier and helped the hundreds of graduating seniors in years to follow make better decisions because of what they had observed about consequences.

Thirty-five members of the Class of 1999 did not go to their senior prom, awards, or senior night. Some were asked to resign from the Honor Society while others had scholarship awards rescinded. One of the students was a class officer and another was my nephew.

As you can imagine, the days to follow were not easy ones, but the respect of the student body, faculty, and most members of the community that I earned for holding my ground would help to define my administration while improving the climate and culture of our school.

NO SECOND-CLASS CITIZENS

All students, regardless of what organizations they belong to, who their friends are, how they dress, or how they wear their hair must be treated with consistency. There will, of course, always be a faction of disenfranchised students who will require additional nurturing to bring around, while some will forever remain recalcitrant.

This is, of course, the case in society as a whole, and thus is not surprising in a school that is a microcosm of that society. This means that the secret of disciplinary success lies in a school leader's ability to bring more disenfranchised students into the fold, knowing that those individuals will, in turn, influence their peers. Young people are most receptive to authority figures who do what they say they will do all of the time, not just when it's convenient and the players involved are less challenging.

School leaders who keep their doors open to all students and listen to their concerns have a better chance of reducing the number of students who are indifferent and simply not invested in the school. Caution must also be exercised when using student leaders, class officers, and student council members to represent the student body on student-centered issues. Remember, there are many students in all of our schools who feel who the most popular, best-looking, most outgoing students are the ones who win the elections, even though they may not be effective leaders. By always turning to the student leaders for student representation, school leaders often alienate the very students they most desire to have represented.

It is my belief that there are teachers in every school who are just as unique, eccentric, and diverse in their interests as those students we can't seem to get vested. Intuitive administrators will capitalize on every opportunity to bring teachers and students with like interests together.

If we have learned anything from the horrific school shootings and suicide pacts that have occurred in our schools in the past, it is that there are school leaders who have let their guard down, allowing students to "fall through the cracks."

Our teachers are constantly reminded to "stop, look, listen, and report" whenever they so much as sense that a student may be in distress or in need of attention.

Issues of inequity and a culture of double standards make the top of the list when identifying practices in school buildings that divide students while causing them to further distance themselves from the vested members of the school community.

An extremely important thing that school leaders do to earn the respect and credibility of their students is to hold all members of the faculty and staff accountable for the same standards of behavior expected of the students. Teachers who are disrespectful toward students or persecute or harass them in any way must suffer the consequences for their impropriety. School leaders must insist that their teachers model the very behavior they expect of their students.

Each time a new semester begins, our teachers are expected to give all students a handout of expected classroom behavior along with their course syllabus. The specific aspects of expected decorum must, however, not contradict our mission or other school policies.

CHAPTER 14

How to Make Difficult Decisions that Are Fair, Objective, and Consistent with the Way You Run Your School

Regardless of how successful a school leader becomes in bettering school culture, improving student learning, raising academic expectations, or making teachers more accountable, stakeholders will forever judge school leaders by their ability to make the tough call.

While there are no magic formulas or generic procedures that will guarantee less stressful or noncontroversial outcomes to those inevitable complex situations that will require a difficult decision, there are a few guiding principles that can help.

These guiding principles, however, can only be applied after a school leader learns to accept some basic truths about how parents, students, colleagues, and significant others will behave when they have something to gain or lose as it relates to a controversial event.

TRUTH OR CONSEQUENCES?

Accept these truths and curtail the consequences.

1. Today's parents will do whatever is necessary to protect their children from having to be accountable or accept consequences for their actions.
2. School administrators have vocal enemies and silent friends. Therefore, never count on anyone coming to your defense.
3. There is no way to depersonalize a controversial situation. Accept the fact that character assassination is the weapon of choice used in combat against school leaders.

4. There is no such thing as a "popular" difficult decision as it applies to school leadership. "When you win, you lose, just as when you lose, you lose."

5. Moral and ethical decisions are a thing of the past. We now live in a litigious society, which requires you to remain focused on your legal responsibilities when making the tough call.

6. The right decision is the decision you make based on your personal convictions. Listen to your conscience and be true to yourself.

7. Delaying the inevitable or avoiding an action that must be taken is caused by fear and will most always result in guilt, increased anxiety, and self-doubt. When you can identify what your fears are grounded to, taking action will help you reduce those fears and give you the confidence to deal with future conflicts.

8. When you take a stand and hold your ground you are sending a message to all those who consider challenging you in the future. The opposition always counts on your giving in to the pressure.

9. No good can ever come from reversing a decision. If a higher authority wants a decision reversed, make it clear that you will do so with the understanding that it was by directive, not choice.

10. The only way to effectively deal with the mistrust that school leaders have come to endure is to trust those few individuals who will never sell you out. Therefore, you must refrain from rationalizing your position on difficult issues, as what you say will be misconstrued and used against you. Keep friends close, but your enemies even closer.

THE THREE P'S

If you can accept the ten basic truths of making difficult decisions, then you can use these guiding principles to help you make decisions that have a basis, follow a logical process, and do not leave you vulnerable or contradict your leadership style.

1. Identify a precedent—When confronted with a situation that will require your action, reflect on similar situations that you have dealt with in the past. Reexamine your former actions and proceed accordingly. If you do not have a precedent, keep in mind

that the decision you make will establish a precedent that you will need to commit to thereafter. Resist following precedents established by former administrators unless they are consistent with your leadership style and methods.

2. Go by the Book—Make your decisions based on the procedures and regulations that are outlined in your Student/Parent Handbook, district manual, or state regulatory manual. The most common mistakes in decision making made by veteran and inexperienced school leaders alike involve misapplication of rules and procedures. Not surprisingly, a single incident of this nature can lead to the ruination of an administrator's career.

3. Pre-assess the Impact—Once you have established what you can and can't do based on the "3 P's" —precedent, policies, and procedures, a thorough assessment of the various ramifications of the different actions you can choose will help lead you to make the right decision and properly deal with the fallout.

ASK YOURSELF THESE QUESTIONS

- Which choice is in the best interest of the study body as a whole?
- If your choice will most likely get the attention of the media, how will you respond to questions? Will it be better to make no comment?
- Should you ask the superintendent or key members of the school board where they stand on the choice you want to make or are you confident that you have covered all the bases?
- Is it necessary for you to make a specific choice that will cause you major stress or discomfort? If so, you need to prepare yourself for the aftermath.
- Are you leaning toward a choice that will be easier for you to deal with but will cause you to lose some credibility? These are the most difficult situations that require the greatest amount of soul searching.

HOW TO DEVELOP A SUPPORT STAFF THAT BECOMES THE GLUE THAT HOLDS YOUR SCHOOL TOGETHER

One of the most important, yet underrated, aspects of a successful school can be identified in the functioning of a support staff composed of hardworking individuals who do their jobs well while making things easier for the students, faculty, and administration. Secretaries, receptionists, office managers, cafeteria workers, and custodians are often taken for granted and seldom rewarded for their efforts, upon which schools are dependent in order to function.

The way in which support staff personnel conduct themselves in the school building is a significant factor as it relates to school culture. If these individuals are treated like second-class citizens, then they will give you a second-rate effort. On the other hand, if administrators insist that the staff be given the same respect as all constituents, and demonstrates this through action, not words, then more often than not, these people will go the extra mile for you.

I have never met a school administrator who ran a good school that did not cultivate and nurture his support staff in an effort to improve school culture and improve efficiency in the daily business of the school.

While some school leaders, who are elitists, need their support personnel to know "they are the boss" and demonstrate this by downgrading them, there are others who literally negotiate with staff members to get them to do things. In both cases, you have leaders with credibility problems and a school culture that will reflect this weakness.

There are a number of stereotypes that we have come to identify among our dysfunctional staff workers. They include the head custodian who behaves like an acting superintendent, the lunch lady who forgot how to smile, the secretary who's always out to lunch, the receptionist who tells parents to come or call back later, and the hall monitor who wanted to be a cop but failed out of the Police Academy.

If you have any of these people on your staffs, it should be only because you inherited them and that you are in the process of seeing that they get early retirement. Keep in mind that these individuals are as they are, and they got that way because they have been enabled to act as they have been made to feel.

Building a support staff that functions as part of your team requires the same amount of work and attention you give to the development of your teaching staff. The more difficult task, however, will involve your efforts in ensuring that faculty and staff work in harmony.

One of the most important things a school leader can do on route to developing an "all-star" staff is to get to know all staff members personally.

Spend time with them, exchange laughs and pleasantries, but more importantly, listen to their concerns and suggestions.

I have always believed that a school leader, or any CEO for that matter, is only as good as his staff. After nine years as a school administrator, this remains my fundamental belief. More importantly, living by this philosophy has allowed me to enjoy the benefits of a talented hardworking staff who have helped to make us a better school.

An administrator may feel, as I do, that he has an outstanding support staff, or may believe that this is an aspect of the school culture that needs work. Regardless of your particular stance, it is beneficial for all of us to be reflective and introspective regarding our staff development practices.

The process begins with a staff assessment that centers on a number of questions. By asking these questions, you can gain the information you need to accentuate your strengths and improve on your weaknesses. (See table 14.1.) It is critical that you involve significant others, like coworkers, parents, students, and members of your Parent Teacher Organization or school council in the process, so that the results of your assessment are objectively analyzed and that improvement initiatives follow.

Replace Secretaries with Office Managers

When education reform reared its demanding head, school administrators, who at one time were exclusively responsible for educational matters, were now responsible for everything from hiring school personnel to teach and plumbers to fix a leaking faucet. Advances in technology, the entitlement of parents to threaten and abuse school leaders, coupled with the demand for accountability reports, newsletters, and legal issues, have made secretaries obsolete. If your personal assistant is still taking dictation or transcribing letters from voice recordings or stenography, then you must be in "Pleasantville." Hopefully, you have been fortunate enough to have an assistant like mine, who deserves to be called an office manager.

My office manager is a multitalented, intuitive, intelligent workhorse, who is skilled in technology, but more importantly, has vast knowledge of human psychology. She is my personal confidante, resident therapist, and the person who most often keeps me out of trouble. Dee's organizational skills are immense, she is forever pleasant and

Table 14.1.   Staff Assessment Survey

Administer to all members of support staff.

		1	2	3	4
1	My immediate work environment is pleasant and comfortable.				
2	My immediate supervisor is fair, honest, reasonable, and respectful.				
3	I am treated by the school faculty with respect and dignity.				
4	I am, for the most part, respected by the students.				
5	When I have concerns, my supervisor and administrators listen and are helpful to me.				
6	Some of my coworkers are given preferential treatment from my immediate supervisor.				
7	The school administration includes us in recreational activities, and appropriate meeting and other collegial activities.				
8	The principal is appreciative of my efforts and makes me feel like a regular member of the staff.				
9	The administration takes a hard line on students who disrespect staff members.				
10	The administration and/or my supervisor are clear in their expectations of me and the job I am assigned to do.				
11	My coworkers are helpful, friendly, and enjoyable to work with.				
12	My immediate supervisor frequently compliments me for a job well done and privately offers me constructive criticism when my performance warrants it.				
13	I feel safe in the school.				
14	I feel that the principal appreciates and values his support staff.				
15	The principal demands that his staff workers behave in the same manner in which his faculty members are expected to behave.				
16	The school board and central administration are sensitive to my needs and appreciative of my efforts.				
17	The superintendent gives the principal and my immediate supervisor the authority to supervise me without interference.				
18	The school board and superintendent support the efforts of the principal in providing the resources and procedures needed for me to do my job efficiently.				
19	Parents and other members of the community treat me with respect and are appreciative of the services I provide the school and their children.				
20	The job I do for the school system is personally rewarding and the wages I am paid are fair and competitive with other school districts.				

1 Always   2 Mostly   3 Sometimes   4 Never

kind, but at the same time she won't take any grief. I have come to find that I am as protective of her as my own wife and children because of the good human being that she is. It goes without saying that she is loyal, conscientious almost to a fault, and exceptionally efficient at keeping me on task. She does this while at the same time performing more daily functions than any other person in the building except my two assistants and their office managers. Not to mention, she knows how to handle oppositional, demanding parents and dysfunctional, uncooperative faculty members.

These are the critical functions that are performed by office managers who can get the job done day in and day out while feeling the same stress that you do.

If you do not have an office manager like mine, it is likely to be because you have been unwilling to relinquish control and put your trust in the one individual who knows more about some aspects of your job that you do.

Inclusion, as It Applies to Staff

School leaders hold a number of meetings and social gatherings each year where they forget, or simply don't include, support staff. By assigning a teacher in your building to assume the role of "social director," you can be sure that each and every member of your team will be "fully included" in all activities.

Also, if you are fortunate enough to have a cafeteria director who doubles as a stand-up comedian, or at least is pleasant, open, and friendly, you can be sure that every day spent in the cafeteria will be a good experience. It is a double bonus when the food being served is first rate, and offers variety, weekly specials, and themes for every holiday. If you come to our cafeteria, it is a guarantee that you will eat well and have a few laughs. Furthermore, all of your social functions will be properly catered without your doing a thing. All you have to do is pay the bill.

Here is a list of a few social events that have helped bond faculty and staff together:

- Scrap the boring faculty meeting and treat your people to a concert. Serve coffee, tea, fruit, pastry, and whatever else makes them smile.
- Hold a 50/50 raffle every Friday. Buy door prizes for faculty/staff meetings from the kitty.
- Hire a motor coach and spend a night at the racetrack or casino. Snacks and drinks on the bus are included.

- Purchase team jerseys (good quality) and have faculty and staff dress in them for a team picture that will be proudly displayed outside your office.
- Put together a faculty/staff basketball team (stacked with athletes) and challenge other schools in your district.

Reward Desired Behavior

Get the "fish hooks" out of your pants pockets and pull out the plastic; in-service days are the perfect opportunity to send your most dedicated office managers out to lunch. Don't be afraid to give them the old credit card, as they are too appreciative of your gesture to run up a big tab. (If you have a martini drinker in the bunch, pick a day that she's absent before you offer to pick up the tab.)

Custodians will generally be appreciative of a couple of pizzas and a dozen doughnuts here and there. (Be careful with the high fat treats if you have guys on the staff named Sal or Pauly as there may be cholesterol issues.)

Make the Rounds

Frequently tour your building, making strategic stops at office stations, the custodial room, and the cafeteria. Do these rounds when you need to get away from the office as it will be good for your staff to see you and much better for you to stay out of the fire.

Excellence Awards

Hand out Excellence Awards in abundance. A pin or a certificate will do. What is more important is that the good things these people do in the building (that bring few rewards) are acknowledged and celebrated in front of the entire assembly of school personnel.

How to Develop a School Culture that Reduces Discipline Problems and Enhances Safety

RECOMMENDED DETERRENTS

- Video surveillance cameras (building and grounds).
- Use of alcohol detention devices at dances, proms, and other co-curricular activities.
- Establish a dress code that prohibits specific articles of clothing.
- Hold parents accountable for the behavior of their children.
- Develop a nonschool conduct policy with "teeth."
- Establish a "three strikes you're out" policy for habitual school offenders.
- Take a hard line on cheating and plagiarism.
- Earn the trust and respect of your students by demonstrating to them that there are no second-class citizens in the school.
- Demonstrate to teachers that they must be accountable for their behavior and actions in the same manner that their students are.
- Develop a character education program that meets the needs of your school culture.
- Develop a peer mediation program, train students to mediate student/student conflicts.
- Do not tolerate abusive, vulgar, or threatening students—give no second chances.
- Hold athletic coaches and activity advisors accountable for how students behave when under their supervision. They need to understand that behavioral expectations apply for all "school-sponsored activities," regardless of whether or not they occur in or out of the building.

- Use canine surveillance to keep drugs out of your school and off campus.
- Search students whenever you suspect they may be holding anything that is in violation of school policy.
- Take an existing position and reconstruct it to be a "security/attendance" monitor position.

How to Deal More Effectively with Difficult Parents

1. Never give a hostile, threatening parent an audience; insist that they remain dignified and civil.
2. Meet with oppositional parents on your terms, but only after you have all the facts and have time to prepare.
3. If the parent has issues with a faculty or staff member, make sure that person is present when you meet with the parent.
4. Never meet with a parent who is represented by legal counsel unless you have legal counsel to represent you.
5. Do not allow a parent to get you to talk about another student or parent under any circumstances.
6. Take notes during meetings with difficult parents and always have one of your assistants present to confirm any and all charges, statements, allegations, etc.
7. Insist that parents make complaints to you in writing and remain focused on the facts.
8. Avoid speaking to volatile, emotional parents on the telephone. Insist that they meet with you in person on your terms.
9. Do not avoid a difficult parent. Return all phone calls and "listen" if they will speak to you in a dignified and civil manner.
10. Abruptly end all meetings that have gone bad and cannot succeed, and if need be, walk out.
11. Refrain from telling parents who clearly are "enablers" what they should or shouldn't be doing with their children as they will use these judgments against you.
12. Stick by the book. The language of your Student/Parent Handbook should be your guide in all controversial matters.

13. Do not succumb to threats or allow a difficult parent to pressure you into reversing a decision you have made with conviction. Let the parent appeal to the superintendent and school board, but be sure your superiors know the facts and are prepared to hear the appeal.

14. Never allow a parent to interview other students or have students other than their own children present at meetings. At all costs protect the confidentiality of your sources of information. They may, however, present you with written statements from other students.

15. Play "good cop, bad cop" with your assistants so as to never compromise the integrity of your leadership team. If an assistant mishandles a situation that leaves him at the mercy of a difficult parent, explain to him the strategy you will employ to get him off the hot seat.

16. Go to the wall for a good teacher who is clearly "in the right." Do not defend the teacher who was irresponsible; when this happens, a difficult parent is suddenly less difficult.

17. Insist that parents follow the "chain of command."

18. If you are a principal, make sure your assistants confer with you prior to dealing with situations that will invariably result in unhappy parents. If you are an assistant, never make a tough decision without first consulting the principal.

Make sure your office staff understands the importance of confidentiality where parents are concerned. "Talking out of school" is the kiss of death.

How to Deal with Difficult Teachers

1. Develop a faculty manual that clearly spells out each responsibility of and expectation for teachers. Be sure to leave no gray areas. This will become the basis for identifying the specific behaviors you need to deal with.
2. Remove or minimize those forums that allow negative, unhappy teachers to spread their poison. Faculty lounges, faculty meetings, and unstructured department gatherings are obvious breeding grounds.
3. Demand that teachers with issues about the way your school is run and who are granted an audience can offer proposed solutions to what they perceive as problems.
4. Reward your good soldiers by accommodating them with regularity. This will allow you to further isolate your problem teachers who will have fewer colleagues with whom to commiserate.
5. Shield your young, enthusiastic, energetic teachers from those problem teachers who will invariably attempt to control, sour, and use them.
6. Be conscious of alienating union representatives who will be more willing to spend time defending problem teachers if they perceive you as aloof and unapproachable.
7. When conferencing with a difficult teacher, stick to the facts and do not allow yourself to be baited into a discussion on personal differences.

8. Flex your muscles, when necessary, and never allow your authority to be challenged. A teacher who thinks he got the better of you will make sure his venomous peers know how he put you in your place.

9. Follow up all discussions with difficult teachers with a memorandum, which restates your expectations. Copy the memorandum to assistants and the superintendent to further confirm your authority. Matters of a more serious nature should be copied to the superintendent with a recommendation that the memorandum be placed in the teacher's personnel file.

10. Don't wait for a problem teacher to demand that he has a union representative present. Instead, tell him you recommend that he has one present when you meet. When these meetings occur, make sure you have a representative of your administrative team present.

11. Ask parents who have complaints about teachers to place them in writing. In turn, require the teacher respond to you in writing in response to the allegations. If the teacher fails to take responsibility, call the parents in, place the teacher in the meeting, and sit back and moderate the proceedings.

12. Make clear to a teacher who chooses to bash you in and out of the school community that he is insubordinate and regardless of the language of the contract, you can discipline him for "conduct unbecoming a professional."

13. By disciplining a single difficult teacher you can change the behavior of numerous others. Never forego an opportunity to send a message.

14. Teachers who bully and harass students should be treated in the same manner. Never be afraid to give them a taste of their own medicine.

15. Teachers, like students, have entitlements by law. They also enjoy privileges that you reserve the right to remove when you see fit. Reassignments, relocations, changes in schedules, supervisory duties, etc., are the very weapons you use to recondition noncompliant teachers.

DIFFERENTIATED INSTRUCTION FOR DIFFICULT TEACHERS

"The Fireside Chat"
"The I Don't Like You Either Assertion"
"The Memorandum of Concern"
"The Personal Improvement Plan"
"The Early Retirement Incentive"
"The Change is Good Double-Double"
"The You're So Talented You Need to Teach Our Most Challenging
    Students Reward"
"The Mini Vacation without Pay"
"The Informal Observation"
"The Evaluation from Hell"
"The Implosion Therapy"
"The Existential Approach"
"The You'd Be Happy Elsewhere" Recommendation

Difficult students, teachers, and parents multiply when the culture of the school and the school's leadership reveal inconsistencies and contradictions in the treatment of the various stakeholders.

By changing the culture, you will greatly reduce the number of problem individuals and the difficulties they bring.

How to Achieve Success with the Next Level of Student Discipline

1. Do not be intimated: stay focused on doing the right thing, stand your ground.
2. Do not allow yourself to become the victim.
3. Learn the difference between "reasonable suspicion" and "probable cause."
4. Review, edit, and revise your Student/Parent Handbook until all gray areas are removed and procedures for all behavioral matters are spelled out clearly.
5. Do not wait for the inevitable: rehearse, simulate, anticipate.
6. Become proactive to reduce your need to be reactive.
7. Refuse to be an island: enlist the support of your faculty, school council, students, and other agencies in the community to gain needed advocacy, insulation, and support.
8. Spend time with your assistants: provide all necessary mentoring, professional development, and case study information to allow them to become experts in school law.
9. Understand the meaning and importance of "due process" where students are concerned.
10. Run your school as a "limited open forum" for students to exercise First Amendment rights and you will waste little time with civil rights matters and the ACLU.
11. Understand that there is, in fact, a relationship between the way young people dress and how they behave.
12. Refuse to spend 75 percent of your time on a handful of oppositional students: a change in attitude is the first step.

13. If you do not have a memorandum of understanding with the local police department, develop one immediately.

14. Learn the value of the general charge of "disruption of school assembly," use juvenile and police officers to remove oppositional, disruptive students from school property.

15. Learn the value and need for "manifestation determinations" when dealing with disciplining students with IEPs and 504 plans.

16. Learn the value of using Children in Need of Services, Parents in Need of Services, and Habitual School Offender petitions in gaining court advocacy for dealing with students and families who will not conform to school policies and procedures.

17. Do not fall on the sword: never fail to document all matters that could prove troublesome.

18. Never make deals with students or parents as they will always come back to bite you.

19. Become a Vulcan: do not be drawn in by parents and students who deliberately try to push your buttons; remain rational and unemotional.

Establish a relationship with a legal advisor who is well versed on school law.

Developing an Administrator-Friendly Student/Parent Handbook

1. Is your handbook revised yearly?
2. Does a committee consisting of teachers, parents, and administrators make recommendations for handbook revisions?
3. Is the handbook reviewed with students at the beginning of each new school year prior to the students' signing off that they have received it?
4. Does your school council endorse all recommendations for handbook revisions prior to their going to the school committee for approval?
5. Is the student leadership council involved in the handbook revision process?
6. Are policies and procedures written clearly so that students, parents, and lawyers can't find "loopholes" where accountability is concerned?
7. Do school administrators and teachers know the law regarding students' rights and due process?

- Reasonable suspicions versus probable cause.
- Grounds for search and seizure.
- Schools as limited open forums for self-expression.
- Entitlements versus privileges.
- Nonschool conduct.
- Exclusionary offenses.
- Suspending students who have IEPs or 504 plans and manifestation determination hearings.

- Superintendent and school committee role in the appeal process.
- Protocol for handbook addendums during the school year.
- Imposing fines for smoking and possession of tobacco products.
- Differences in the rights of seventeen- and eighteen-year-old students versus minors.
- Parental accountability for habitual school offenders.
- CHINS petitions.
- Restraining orders.
- Issuing letters of no trespass.
- Using alcohol detection devices.
- Dress code.
- Using town counsel in legal matters.
- Memorandums of understanding with local police department.
- Using canines for drug surveillance of lockers and cars parked on school grounds.
- Local (town) laws and ordinances in conflict with school policies and procedures.
- Authority of police and juvenile officers in the school.
- Noncustodial parent rights.

Seven Reasons Why School Administrators Cannot Turn Their Backs on Issues of Non-school Conduct

1. Volatile issues between students that occur outside of school will almost always continue in school, impacting school climate, disrupting the learning environment, and compromising the safety of students, faculty, and staff.

2. The mission of almost all schools includes teaching students how to behave responsibly. We cannot be true to a mission that holds students accountable only for the way they behave during school hours and at school-sponsored activities.

3. Student leaders, athletes, and members of the National Honor Society who live by the standards and honor codes required by their organizations need our leadership and conviction to stay the course. We vindicate and reinforce the values of these young people when we remove the privilege of membership from their peers who behave irresponsibly.

4. When students realize that they can, in fact, be held accountable for nonschool conduct, we increase the odds of having students consider the consequences before acting irresponsibly or in a manner that may put them or others at risk.

5. Educating young people who are often misled by irresponsible parents and a culture that glorifies risky behavior is a reality of the job we have chosen and are compensated to do. If we refuse to accept this challenge, then we become part of the problem.

6. Almost all school tragedies resulting in the loss of life could be prevented if educators became involved in the lives of their students as they did in years past when the so-called "disenfranchised" student

was more easily identified. We must restore the faith of our teachers in our honesty and purpose and regain their confidence that we will protect them from reprisals when they share with us important information about students as it pertains to what they are doing out of school.

A school administration that is respected by the general student population, their parents, and the community as a whole is defined by its ability to do the right thing regardless of who is involved. Doing the right thing requires that administrators act on the information provided to them in matters wherein nonschool conduct is concerned, no matter how difficult the circumstances.

You Make the Call

The following scenarios involve situations that forced me to make some very tough calls. Using any precedents, your school handbook, district manual, and/or state policy manual, determine what you would do and what impact your decision(s) would have.

SCENARIO 1

While searching a student for cigarettes, your assistant principal finds a small bag of marijuana in a female student's pocketbook. She tells him she is holding it for a friend. She also has prescription pain killers that belong to her mother.

SCENARIO 2

Prior to senior week, the senior class was told that if they were caught drinking in the community, they would lose their senior privileges (prom, awards, senior night). The night before the seniors' last day, forty-two class members were arrested for illegal possession of alcohol. One of the students was your nephew and another the class secretary and daughter of a school board member. The arrests were made the night before the seniors' last day of school and prior to the senior prom, senior awards night, senior class night, and graduation.

SCENARIO 3

A weekend party at a home in your community resulted in the house being badly damaged. You receive the police report indicating that there was drinking, but none of your students were arrested for drinking. The students charged with doing damage to the home gave police names of other students who were involved. Your assistant principals interview a number of students and some admit to being there while others deny it. Some say they were drinking, while others say they stopped by but left when they saw what was happening. Your assistants confirm that ten students active in season athletics were present at the party but only five admitted to drinking and to doing any damage. Three of the ten were also members of the National Honor Society.

SCENARIO 4

One of your teachers reports to your assistant principal that a student reeks of marijuana. Your assistant calls the student down and searches him. The student has nothing in his possession and denies smoking marijuana. The school nurse is asked to examine the student and she feels he was, in fact, under the influence. The parents of the student are called to the school to pick the student up. They claim that their son should not have been questioned or searched without their consent because he was only fifteen years old. They threaten to sue the school if he is disciplined.

SCENARIO 5

A female student reports to you that one of her teachers patted her on the rear end while attempting to move her from the corridor into his classroom. The student, in a written statement, claimed that she was humiliated and made uncomfortable by the teacher. The teacher did not deny the allegation but said he was only kidding around with the student. The teacher had no prior complaints leveled against him from other students in his fifteen-year tenure at your school.

SCENARIO 6

A teacher is told by one of her students that four members of her class stole a copy of her final exam from her desk. The teacher heard of this after the exam was graded and the final grades were posted. The exam was given on the last day of school and the four students involved, all juniors, were now on summer vacation. The teacher believed that her exam was, in fact, stolen and that most members of her class were aware of it. Three of the four members accused of the theft were members of the National Honor Society, one was the son of a faculty member, and all four were fall sport varsity athletes.

SCENARIO 7

Four varsity cheerleaders reported that they were on an Internet chat room with three freshman boys from your school and that threats were made indicating that the cheerleaders would be shot and killed at a future home basketball game. The parents of the cheerleaders went to the police and told school administrators that they were keeping their daughters home because they did not feel safe in school. When interviewed by police and school officials, the boys denied making the threats. The incident was reported two days prior to the Christmas break and was sensationalized in the newspaper and on television.

SCENARIO 8

A student reported to the assistant principal that a senior boy was selling drugs from his car which was parked on school grounds. It was the senior boy's last day of school and he had successfully completed all of his classwork to be eligible to graduate. As the principal of the school, you called in your juvenile officer to assist you in the search of the boy's vehicle. The boy was called down to your office and confronted with the allegations, which he denied were true. As you left your office with the boy and your juvenile officer to perform the search of his vehicle, the boy bolted, sprinting to his vehicle and drove away recklessly at high speed. While leaving the school grounds he nearly caused a serious accident.

When the father of the boy was contacted by you, he threatened to secure a lawyer and sue the school if his son, who he claimed ran out of fear, was disciplined.

SCENARIO 9

A popular student athlete from a well-known home in the community meets the academic and service requirements for National Honor Society. A couple of reports of character unbecoming a candidate by teachers in the school result in his not being selected. The boy and his parents demand a hearing with the advisors and members of the teacher's selection board. They also demand that all negative reports regarding their son be disclosed to them.

SCENARIO 10

A parent calls to inform you that his son was "paddled" with a wooden board kept in the football locker room and used traditionally by upperclassmen on the team to initiate younger members of the team into the football fraternity. In your investigation into the matter, you learn that it was in fact true but that your coaches were not aware of it. You also discover that key members of the team were responsible. The team plays a big game on Friday, and by Thursday you have some team members who have admitted their involvement, but others whom you believe are involved based on information provided to you are denying any involvement.

SCENARIO 11

One of your veteran teachers, who is a good classroom teacher, is a negative, vocal member of the faculty who has a tendency to "talk out of school." You have received a number of complaints from parents that they are concerned about this teacher's tendency to talk to others about their children. In your written evaluation of the teacher, you indicate your concerns regarding breaches of confidentiality and chronic negativity. On receipt of your evaluation, the teacher becomes offended, claims there are no such indications in any other evaluations, and demands that your comments be removed from the evaluation.

SCENARIO 12

Two boys in your school have an ongoing conflict that has resulted in numerous incidents between them. Both of the boys' families are literally at war and are in and out of the school making demands on administration to see their point of view. One afternoon, after school hours, in a student parking lot, a black sedan arrives with a rather sizable individual, apparently a relative of one of the boys. He proceeds to deliver a beating to his cousin's schoolboy enemy, gets in the car, and is driven away. The police are called and a complaint is filed. The next day, the father of the boy who was beaten arrives at school and demands that the boy who "ordered" the beating on his son be suspended from school.

SCENARIO 13

A fifteen-year-old student, on an IEP, is charged by the police for committing a felony outside of school. His case will not be heard in the courts for months to come. It is your belief, based on the charges, that the student's presence in your school makes other students feel uncomfortable and unsafe.

SCENARIO 14

Two of your teachers retire in the same year that the school district endures extreme budget cuts. A number of teaching positions are eliminated, but the two positions you have available will be filled. During the summer vacation, the superintendent, without consulting you, fills your vacancies with two middle school teachers in the system who were bumped out of their positions by teachers with more seniority. One of these teachers was certified in business but placed in a social studies position. The other was certified in the English position she was assigned to, but neither teacher had any teaching experience at the high school level.

SCENARIO 15

A student whom you believe is in possession of drugs is called to the assistant principal's office and confronted with the allegation. Fearing that he would be searched, the student reaches into his pocket, removes the drugs, stuffs them in his mouth, and proceeds to chew and swallow them.

SCENARIO 16

A student tells another student that he has a gun and that he's going to use it in the cafeteria during lunch. The statement is made from stall to stall in one of the boy's lavatories and neither boy has seen the other. The boy who hears the threat leaves the lavatory and goes back to class to tell his peers. One of his peers goes right to one of the assistant principals who immediately replays the video surveillance tape made available from the camera placed outside of the lavatory. The boy making the gun threats is positively identified, the police are called, and the boy is questioned. The boy denies making any such statements. Meanwhile, the rumor has spread throughout the school and your students and faculty are in a panic.

SCENARIO 17

Two students are engaged in a violent fistfight in a school corridor. A male faculty member, while attempting to break up the fracas, is injured. The same student who started the fight, according to witnesses, was the one who caused the injury to the faculty member. The faculty member sustains a broken thumb and files a police report charging the student with assault and battery.

SCENARIO 18

A student, who regularly wears a trench coat to school frequently loiters in front of a teacher's classroom during nonclass hours. The teacher reports to an assistant principal that the boy makes her nervous and uncomfortable. The boy is told to remove his trench coat and to keep it in his locker during school hours. The boy refuses and is supported by his parents who claim the school dress code does not prohibit trench coats.

SCENARIO 19

A teacher becomes enraged when she is hit by a flying object while teaching class. The boy whom she claims threw the object at her is removed from class. The following day your assistant principal reads the discipline report, and after the boy claims he was not responsible, he asks the teacher, if she is 100 percent sure of what she witnessed. The teacher is insulted that she is even questioned and the boy is suspended for three days. The next day, three students from the class report that while the teacher had her back to the board, the student she claimed hit her with an object, was playing with his pen and the top flew off and accidentally hit the teacher.

SCENARIO 20

A senior boy on an IEP causes the school to be evacuated when he pulls a fire alarm box during school hours. The boy is turned in by students who witnessed the act. The boy is suspended for the maximum ten days and a manifestation determination meeting is held at the conclusion of the suspension. As principal of the school you plan on excluding the student. At the manifestation hearing, the team determines that the boy's behavior was in fact "impulsive" as was stated in his IEP, but the boy tells the team that he knew exactly what he was doing when he pulled the alarm.

References

Bulach, C.R., Lunenburg, F.C., & McCallon, R. (1995). *The influence of the principal's leadership style on school climate and student achievement. People in Education*, 3(3), 333–350.

Clarke, J.H., & Frazer, E. (2003). Making learning personal: Educational practices that work. In J. DiMartino, J. Clarke, & D. Wolk (Eds.), *Personalized learning: Preparing high school students to create their futures*. Lanham, MD: Scarectow Press.

Dalziel, M.M., & Schoonover, S.C. (1988), *Changing ways: A practical tool for implementing change within organizations*. New York: Amacom.

Fullan, M.G. (with S. Stiegelbauer). (1991). *The new meaning of educational change*. New York: Teachers College Press.

Gainey, D.D., & Webb, L.D. (1998). *The education leader's role in change: How to proceed*. Reston, VA: National Association of Secondary School Principals.

National Association of Secondary School Principals. (1996), *Breaking ranks: Changing an American institution*. Reston, VA: Author.

National Association of Secondary School Principals. (1998). *Breaking ranks leadership: A development program for school teams*. Reston, VA: Author.

National Commission on Excellence in Education. (1983). *A nation at risk: The imperative for educational reform*. Washington, DC: U.S. Government Printing Office.

Painter, B., & Valentine, J. (1999). *Engaging teachers in the school improvement process*. Reston, VA: National Association of Secondary School Principals.

Phillips, G., & Wagner, C. (2003). *School culture assessment*. Vancouver, British Columbia: Agent 5 Design.

Robbins, P., & Alvy, H. (1995). *The principal's companion*. Thousand Oaks, CA: Corwin Press.

Webb, L.D., and Norton, F.S. (1999). *Human resources administration: Personal needs and issues in personnel administration* (3rd ed.). New York: Prentice Hall.

About the Author

John M. Brucato is the principal of Milford High School, Milford, Massachusetts. He is a former assistant principal, teacher, coach, dean of students, and activity advisor. An active member of the Massachusetts Interscholastic Athletic Association and member of the Massachusetts Secondary School Administrators Association Board of Directors, Mr. Brucato has presented numerous workshops on various educational issues related to school leadership and culture.

In addition to developing a number of graduate courses for secondary school educators, Mr. Brucato coauthored "Questions and Answers About Block Scheduling," *Eye on Education*, 1999, and has consulted with over twenty schools in Massachusetts, Vermont, New Hampshire, New York, Rhode Island, and New Jersey. Mr. Brucato, who was recently named a distinguished educator by the Massachusetts Department of Education, has participated in various educational debates on local television, CNN, Fox News, and Boston Public Television.